ENJOY THE GRIND

HOW TO NAVIGATE STRESS, MASTER YOUR MINDSET, AND CREATE HAPPINESS IN YOUR TWENTIES

JOE VAN GEISON

Enjoy the Grind: How to Navigate Stress, Master Your Mindset, and Create Happiness in Your Twenties

Joe Van Geison

Copyright © 2022 JVG LLC

All Rights Reserved.

No part of this publication may be reproduced, distributed, or transmitted in any form or by any means, including photocopying, recording, or other electronic or mechanical methods, without the prior written permission of the publisher, except in the case of brief quotations embodied in critical reviews and certain other noncommercial uses permitted by copyright law.

Disclaimer: The author makes no guarantees concerning the level of success you may experience by following the advice and strategies contained in this book, and you accept the risk that results will differ for each individual. The purpose of this book is to educate, entertain, and inspire.

Print ISBN: 979-8-9872268-0-3

CONTENTS

Enjoy the Grind Online   v
The Grind Redefined   xi

The 18 Disciplines   1

PART ONE
MINDSET
Love Yourself   9
Find Your Focus   18
Choose Joy   26
Always Be Teachable   35
Work For Future You   43

PART TWO
ROUTINES
Master Motivation   53
Win The Day   62
Hang The Lights   69
Look For Lay-Ups   73
Rise And Grind   78
Respect Your Body   87
Reflect Every Week   96

PART THREE
LIFESTYLE
Celebrate Success   105
Meet Your Money   111
Think Like A Peak Performer   117
Feel Good Now   126
Connect With Community   135
Finish What You Start   142

Hit The Road   148

Notes	151
Acknowledgments	155
About the Author	157

ENJOY THE GRIND ONLINE

In an effort to enhance your experience, we have created a one-stop shop for you to access all of the recommended resources mentioned in the following pages. This way you can easily connect with me, download activities, and view a full list of resources all in one place.

Access the Enjoy the Grind Online Experience Here: bit.ly/enjoy-the-grind

The unique online experience will also give you free bonuses, such as continued support through my Enjoy the Grind newsletter, and additional motivational and educational video content!

I can't wait to connect and support you along your journey.

Your Friend,

To have Joe speak at your team or organization's next event, order bulk copies of *Enjoy the Grind* at a discounted rate, or to receive one-on-one coaching, please email Joe and his team at **jvgfindyourfocus@gmail.com** or visit him on the web at **www.focussolutionscoaching.com**.

"It is not in the pursuit of happiness that we find fulfillment,
it is in the happiness of pursuit."
—Denis Waitley

Dedicated to all the young professionals and college students who want to reach their highest potential and enjoy life in the process. You can be happy and successful at the same time, and you deserve both.

THE GRIND REDEFINED
INTRODUCTION

"You do not find the happy life, you make it."

CAMILLA EYRING KIMBALL

Let's talk about it . . .

You recently graduated from college and you just landed your first *real* job. You have a salary, health benefits, and a legitimate life update at your next family gathering.

YOU have arrived!

What if, regardless of the horror stories you have been told, you could fall in love with your first "real-world" job? What if you had a road map of how to make the most of this time in your career to build an amazingly strong relationship with yourself? What if that road map led you to new levels of happiness that will allow you to become a peak performer?

Whether you want to make big money, get noticed by your boss, or lock in your future dream job, chances are you are looking at your current job as a quick pit stop along the way. A bottomless pit of cold calls and pointless tasks reserved for entry-level employees. Well, my friends, there is another option. This book is intended to shift your perspective on the personal and professional growth you can have in your twenties. If you accept the challenge, I believe that your early twenties can provide you with the critical foundation of self-love and joy necessary to unlock your true potential and years of happiness and high performance.

As a performance coach, sales director, and college administrator throughout the last ten years, I have worked with hundreds of college students and young professionals and have seen firsthand the toll that the "grind" can have on young people. Society popularizes putting happiness aside to trudge through the stress and overwhelm of college and the early stages of our careers with the hopes that one day we can get promoted and *then* start living the life we deserve. Not only have I seen this in my clients and team members, but I have also experienced it in my own life. For the first years of my career, my compass was way off course. I assumed that happiness was on the other side of a new title and a raise, only to continuously battle with stress, overwhelm, and an extremely lopsided work-life balance. In the last few years of my twenties, I flipped the switch and aimed my compass toward joy. And my whole life changed. I found that consistent self-care and experiencing joy on a regular basis led me to identifying my true passions, chasing my dreams, and performing at my very best.

You can struggle through "the grind" with the rest of your peers and find yourself riddled with stress, anxiety, and self-doubt. Or you can *enjoy* the grind and use this time in your life to intentionally explore disciplines that will serve you personally and professionally for years to come!

I believe you deserve the truth, and the fact is that your first job and your early twenties are whatever you make of them. You will get out what you put in. They can be miserable, or they can be a huge opportunity to evolve as a person. I encourage you to see them as the latter. To me, your twenties are a time where you can focus your effort and work extremely hard on a skill that you may not have learned in school. Happiness. That's right, I am a firm believer that happiness is a skill. Just like a musician can improve on the guitar or a quarterback can develop a knack for throwing the perfect pass, you can learn how to create happiness in your own life. Sadly, too many people see happiness as something that we experience—that happens to us—and don't realize it is much more in our control than we realize.

I want to shift the conversation from simply *experiencing* happiness to *creating* happiness for two reasons:

1. I genuinely want people to love the life they live.
2. When we are happy, we perform better.

As a former college Assistant Vice President turned Performance Coach, I have supported hundreds of young people as they navigated their college years and first years in professional life, and the writing is on the wall. If you are not in a healthy, loving relationship with yourself, then you will struggle to perform at your best. To be clear, you can experience financial and professional success and still be miserable. You can perform at an above-average level while being a shell of yourself, but peak performance for you can only be reached when you genuinely enjoy who you are and what you do. As I alluded to before, my goal is to show you that you can be happy and successful no matter how many hours you work or how demanding your job is. Furthermore, I would say that being happy is a key to unlocking higher levels of success!

THE HIGHWAY OF HAPPINESS & HIGH PERFORMANCE

Life is a journey, and in today's world, we are extremely fortunate to enjoy that journey on the wide-open road. We hop in our cars, trucks, and SUVs, and we have the opportunity to enjoy the ride. Not everyone does it, but the opportunity is there. Every person navigates life in their own way. Some cautiously take the back roads while others fly by on the expressway with little regard for the speed limit. Wherever you are in your journey, and however you drive, I encourage you to set your GPS destination to happiness. For the rest of this book, and hopefully the remainder of your life, I want you to use happiness as your guide. By using happiness as your compass, you will know where to go, what turns to make, and what exits to take along the way. This book is a practical roadmap to creating happiness in your own life. My mission in life is to help others find self-love and joy. It is a never-ending journey, but if you visit the right places, you can enjoy the grind much, much sooner.

In my life and in my career, I have made many mistakes, learned a ton from others, and tried to collect as many helpful disciplines as I could to enjoy life more. This book is my way of sharing that collection with you so that you may avoid some of the potholes and dark alleys that I drove through in my twenties.

I have consolidated the eighteen most influential disciplines into one easy-to-digest road map to creating happiness in your life. You can consider each one of these disciplines as a metaphorical stop along the highway of happiness and high performance. Notice that it is the highway *of* happiness, not the highway *to* happiness. Joy can be found in the process, not only in the destination. I am still in the thick of my travels. I still mess up, I still have moments of doubt, I still am learning. But I am beyond excited to learn with you. We get to enjoy the entire journey, from start to finish. Our paths will be different, and we may spend different amounts of time exploring each discipline along the highway. The best part is we get to revisit chapters and take trips back to certain stops to dive back in as we continue to evolve.

Just like in life, once we take the exit ramp to get to a new destination, we are incapable of being physically somewhere else. Being present and focused on where you are each moment is critical to happiness, so when you stop to learn more about disciplines like Choosing Joy or Hanging the Lights, please allow yourself to be there. Be all in as you experience that discipline, and take all that you can from it in those moments. Implement what feels right for you in your life, and then move on to the next exit.

None of these concepts are new, but hearing them again in a different way, at a different time in your life, can lead to new actions and, thus, new results. Sometimes you may just need to stop for gas or a quick bite to eat, and other times you may visit a location for a weekend. The same applies here. If you feel like you have already mastered a certain discipline, then read the chapter, enjoy the reminder, and move on! If you are new to a discipline, then read the chapter, follow the prompts to take action, and give yourself time to build it into your daily routine.

As you implement the following disciplines in your life, they will inevitably lead to more joy, but it is critical that you carve our specific time to do what you love. You have a say in how you feel, so make sure you act accordingly. If you love golfing, then find time to play once a week. If you enjoy hiking and being outdoors, then move to a climate that allows you to be outside.

I realize that what has worked for me, my teams, and my clients may work differently for everyone, so I have done my best to fill every chapter with as many effective concepts, tools, and strategies as possible. This way, you can adopt the tips that you resonate with and move past the tools that don't connect with your lifestyle or personality. Not everything in this book will work for you, but my hope is that you use pieces and suggestions from each discipline as building blocks to create your own peak performance foundation. It is so important that you take ownership of this journey and listen to what feels right and wrong for you. Be patient and prepared to use a healthy dose of grit and grace along the way. The highway of happiness will take time to explore, but I promise it is worth the trip.

EXIT HERE

This book is designed to give you the proper off-ramps to experience each discipline and then get back on the highway of happiness. Each discipline will end with an Exit Here Recap. This way you can easily refresh yourself on the concepts covered and effectively take action. Each exit will have the following elements to best allow you to refer to and utilize the content.

Road Map: Recap of main concepts.

Ask for Directions: Questions you can ask yourself or others that will help give you clarity about where you are in your journey.

Add to Your Playlist: Resources that can help you dig in further to topics and ideas. These can be books, YouTube clips, podcasts, and more.

Pit Stop: Challenges to complete to deepen your understanding and share your trip with others.

HOW TO ENJOY YOUR TRIP

Implementing these disciplines is a commitment to growth, self-discovery, and a pursuit of joy. As you level up, you are going to have to recommit yourself to the same disciplines and

THE GRIND REDEFINED

fight the same battles repeatedly. There were times while writing this book that I doubted these disciplines, but I assure you, they are the reason that it is available for you to read today.

The next section will introduce the disciplines and help you gain a sense of where you are with each. I shared them in the order that makes the most sense to me, but you don't have to visit them in sequential order. Head to the discipline that is calling to you right now and go from there!

Now hop in, crank some feel-good tunes, and let's enjoy the grind!

THE 18 DISCIPLINES

"Discipline yourself and others won't have to."

JOHN WOODEN

When I was in third grade, I was sent to the hall for talking while the teacher was talking. For any eight-year-old, this would have been a negative experience, but in my case, it was worse than that. My dad was a teacher in the building, so I was terrified that he would happen to walk by and see me. I knew if he noticed me in the hallway, I was done for. After what seemed like an eternity, my teacher, Mrs. Burns finally came into the hall and allowed me to rejoin the class. I was a free man. Thank goodness! I breathed a sigh of relief as I snuck back into the classroom, seemingly unscathed from the whole situation.

After school, I met up with my dad like normal and walked with him through the winding hallways and out to the parking lot. He was quieter than usual, but I didn't think much of it. We hopped in our van and headed for home. Or so I thought. Five minutes passed in silence, and I knew something was up. We lived only a mile from the school so it usually only took us two minutes to get home. My anticipation grew as we drove another ten minutes in silence. Clearly, I failed to realize that Mrs. Burns had called my dad while I was in the hallway. Another twenty minutes passed as he contemplated what he was going to say. I don't know if he was giving me the silent treatment on purpose or just trying to build anticipation, but either way it worked. Those felt like the longest minutes of my life. Then finally, as we circled back home and descended the long hill leading to our driveway, he broke the silence. My dad gave me the earful I deserved about respecting Mrs. Burns and how I should not be disruptive in class. He finished his effective educational session by sharing a quote that I would hear many times throughout my life.

"Discipline yourself and others won't have to."

We all know it is important to be disciplined, but the concept of disciplining myself has led to much of my personal and professional growth.

It's good to be motivated by your new boss, or the responsibilities you have to the team, but at the end of the day, you only have yourself. Self-discipline will keep you going when you don't have a project deadline, or your boss isn't encouraging you to be your best. Jocko Willink explains, "discipline equals freedom,"[1] and he is right. And I would add to his philosophy that self-discipline equals joy. Practicing discipline is just setting commitments with yourself and continuously trying your best to keep those commitments. Over and over again, you honor yourself and you see that you are someone who is worth showing up for.

There is a reason this book is filled with eighteen *disciplines*. Not steps, not tips, not habits. These are disciplines because *discipline* implies choice. Discipline implies intention, consistent practice, and implementation over time. To be disciplined, you have to proactively seek out the action that leads to the result you want, and you have to execute accordingly. As mentioned before, this book is about being intentional about creating joy in your life, and the absolute best way I know to do that is through the practice of these disciplines.

PLAN YOUR TRIP

Below you will find a list of the eighteen disciplines of happiness and high performance. I am a firm believer in the process of self-evaluation, so I want to kick things off by sharing the disciplines to give you the opportunity to understand and evaluate where you are in relation to mastering each. The order in which they are listed is a guide that has worked for me and my clients, but I realize that you may have already built some of these disciplines into your daily life. Reviewing the complete list will allow you to see opportunities for growth and make decisions on what you need most right now.

I encourage you to read every chapter, but this will help you get a sense for which chapters will be a quick reminder and which may take a little more time and effort to implement and practice.

THE 18 DISCIPLINES OF HAPPINESS AND HIGH PERFORMANCE

1 | LOVE YOURSELF | I treat myself like my best friend and act accordingly.
2 | FIND YOUR FOCUS | I consistently find opportunities to grow and evolve.
3 | CHOOSE JOY | I intentionally choose to create and experience happiness.
4 | ALWAYS BE TEACHABLE | I am willing to learn and accept change to reach my potential.
5 | WORK FOR FUTURE YOU | I connect my current sacrifices to my future purpose.
6 | MASTER MOTIVATION | I fill my own tank with the fuel of consistent self-motivation.
7 | WIN THE DAY | I avoid procrastination by doing what's most important first.
8 | HANG THE LIGHTS | I take pride in performing mundane tasks at a high level.
9 | LOOK FOR LAY-UPS | I identify and execute small tasks that align with my bigger vision.
10 | RISE AND GRIND | I have a morning and evening routine that sets me up for success.
11 | RESPECT YOUR BODY | I am active every day and eat foods that serve my body.
12 | REFLECT EVERY WEEK | I give myself clarity on what I learn, enjoy, and can improve on.
13 | CELEBRATE SUCCESS | I make time to celebrate big and small wins along my journey.
14 | MEET YOUR MONEY | I have a healthy, positive relationship with my money.
15 | THINK LIKE A PEAK PERFORMER | I treat every day like the biggest day of my life.

16 | FEEL GOOD NOW | I utilize specific strategies to help me feel my best in any situation.
17 | CONNECT WITH COMMUNITY | I reach out to people in my network every day.
18 | FINISH WHAT YOU START | I commit to the right things and am accountable to my word.

PART ONE
MINDSET

LOVE YOURSELF
EXIT 1

"Accept yourself, love yourself, and keep moving forward. If you want to fly, you have to give up what weighs you down."

ROY T. BENNETT

A Lesson from the Sioux:[1]

In ancient times, the Creator wanted to hide something from the humans until they were ready to see it. He gathered all other creatures of creation to ask for their advice.

The eagle said, "Give it to me, and I will take it to the highest mountain in all the land," but the Creator said, "No, one day they will conquer the mountain and find it."

The salmon said, "Leave it with me, and I will hide it at the very bottom of the ocean," but the Creator said, "No, for humans are explorers at heart, and one day they will go there too."

The buffalo said, "I will take it and bury it in the very heart of the Great Plains," but the Creator said, "No, for one day, even the skin of the earth will be ripped open, and they will find it there."

The creatures of creation were stumped, but then an old blind mole spoke up. "Why don't you put it inside them? That's the very last place they'll look."

The Creator said, "It is done."

As this Sioux legend beautifully illustrates, true happiness can only be found from within. Enjoying life can only be possible through discovering inward joy. The foundation of every relationship we have in our lives stems from the relationship we have with ourselves. As we focus on the relationship that we have with happiness, it is imperative that we start with the relationship we have with ourselves. Throughout this book and in life, you are going to be given access to so many resources, disciplines, and tools, but if you don't love yourself, you will never stick to any of them. Self-love and self-care are complicated, but as the Sioux describe in their legendary tale, we must look within to find happiness. We must explore the current relationship that we have with ourselves. Then, and only then, will you be able to create consistent happiness and realize your truest potential. The road to unconditional self-love is an endless one, but to me it is a constant cycle of four elements.

CYCLE OF SELF-LOVE

- **Learn** | Understand who you are right now
- **Accept** | Respect where you are in the moment
- **Decide** | Evaluate your options to move forward with this new information
- **Love** | Act in a way that honors your decision

Learn | Understand Who You Are Right Now

When I start working with a new client, I always start with them taking a personality assessment. This strategy came from my first formal life coach, Shaun, and it really allowed me to make significant changes in my life. Personality tests don't put anyone in a box, or limit their growth potential, and they are a great way to start the journey of self-exploration. If we are interested in evolving and choosing different paths, we must first stop and see what path we are currently on and what tendencies we have now.

Accept | Respect Where You Are in the Moment

As I look back to most of my personal growth and when I evaluate some of my clients' biggest wins, I see they all can be traced back to this Cycle of Self-Love. Some of the most profound "aha" moments with clients have come when they simply take the time to learn about themselves and accept their tendencies and love themselves for who they are. A good amount of frustration doesn't come from who we are or how we act, it comes from a lack of acceptance and self-love surrounding certain actions. For example, I have worked with countless people who hate how much they care about others because it makes them more susceptible to toxic relationships. They would spend time each day hating this about themselves, which is a recipe for disaster if you are trying to be consistently happy. This is where acceptance is critical. Once they accept their caring nature can put them at risk of being hurt, they can be proud of who they are, rather than hate themselves for it. Through acceptance of the "negative," they realize some of the positives that are associated with that tendency. In this example, people who are really caring also tend to have deep, loving, and reciprocal relationships. Instead, they perseverate on the one or two toxic relationships because they haven't yet learned how to deal with them in a healthy way.

Decide | Evaluate Your Options to Move Forward with this New Information

Once we have accepted who we are and love ourselves for it anyway, we have a choice to make. Do we continue to act in the same way or do we adjust how we act to experience a new outcome? Let's continue with the example from earlier and see how this played out for a few of my clients. At this point they have three options. They can (1) continue to put themselves in toxic relationships and hate themselves for it, (2) stop caring about others completely so they can never get hurt again, or (3) continue to care about people and learn strategies to leave toxic relationships and identify warning signs that may help avoid similar scenarios in the future. Now that we are using happiness as our life compass, it becomes clear they must rule out option one to be happy. Through self-awareness, most clients know intuitively that it would be very difficult and less fulfilling to stop caring about others altogether, so the second option also fades away. It can take five minutes or five weeks for people to work through this process of acceptance, but they all come to the same conclusion: the best way to honor themselves is option three, getting better at ending toxic relationships in a healthy way and trying to avoid them in the future. Seeing this is important, but deciding to do something about it is paramount.

Love | Act in a Way that Honors Your Decision

Boy, do I love a good decision. Once we have decided what we want, our options for action become clear. *Love* is an action word. Throughout this Cycle of Self-Love, you have heard words like *honor, accept, decide, change,* and *adjust*. Notice, these are all actions. The best way we can show ourselves love is through action. If you truly want to love yourself, you will act like you love yourself.

MEET YOUR NEW BEST FRIEND

I have had the chance to meet, work with, and present to thousands of people in the last ten years through several avenues. One thing that I have seen over and over is a willingness to treat others better than we treat ourselves. When people ask for advice or troubleshoot a problem, I often ask them to imagine that their best friend is having this issue, and then I ask them to give their friend advice on how to move forward. We need to start showing up for ourselves like we show up for a friend. For example, we build our friends up, and we put ourselves down. We go out of our way to help others and put our own needs to the side. It's important to understand that there is a big difference between caring for yourself and being selfish, and somewhere along the way, society has blurred that line.

In order to reshape the relationship we have with ourselves, we need to first *see* ourselves in a new light. The absolute best way I have found to practice this comes from author and coach, Mel Robbins, and her book *The High Five Habit*. Please take the time to read her book, but here is the premise briefly. Next time you are in front of your mirror, take a few seconds to actually *see* yourself. Look yourself directly in your eyes and high-five the mirror. As Mel notes in her book, this feels a bit weird at first, but the action of giving yourself a high five is exactly why it works. As humans, we have a positive association with giving and receiving high fives. The act of high-fiving yourself in the mirror and actually looking into your eyes is so random that our brain pays extra close attention to the action.[2] Now we have a super positive action that our brain is giving focused attention to. A high five in the morning, or fist bump in the mirror throughout the day, allows us to show up for ourselves in an entirely new way. It lets us *see* ourselves as someone to be celebrated and supported, which opens a ton of doors later on! Look through the bed head, or tired eyes from just waking up, and *see* you. Just give yourself a moment like this, and you will start to *see* yourself as a friend. Once you meet this new friend of yours, treat them like your best friend. Trust me, this one is a game changer.

JUST BE YOU

After years of recruiting and sales, I can promise you success comes through being authentic. If you are a young person trying to be great at sales, then you better get really good at being yourself. Sure, you need to learn the product or service you are sharing with the world, but after you have that basic knowledge, it all boils down to authenticity. People can tell when you are being genuine, and thus they are more likely to buy, and you are more likely to make sales. This is a perfect example of enjoying the grind because not only will you perform better in sales, you will also be able to enjoy the process because you are being your authentic self. Unfortunately, a lot of twenty-to-thirty-year-olds spend their time trying to be someone they aren't to please others, which leads to tension, stress, and unhappiness. The most difficult part is that the people we're trying to please are often the ones closest to us. We act out of alignment to accommodate our parents, friends, and partners. While this is always well intended, it does rob us of happiness and authenticity. Just like a potential buyer who is off put by an inauthentic salesperson, we can tell when we aren't being our genuine selves. Over time, we forget who we are and make a habit of compromising our authenticity.

As you learn more about who you are and see yourself as your own best friend, I want to give you permission to be that person, *all the time*. Throughout my years of coaching college students and young professionals, I noticed most of their problems stem from not being true to themselves. They are passionate about a specific job, but they sacrifice being in alignment by taking the first job offer that comes their way. They move in with a couple friends to save money on rent, when they know they don't like living with other people. They are overwhelmed at work because they can't say no to taking on more projects, even though they hate juggling multiple things. Unfortunately, these decisions that throw us out of alignment are common, and as you engage in the Cycle of Self-Love and strengthen your relationship with yourself, you will notice that you spend a good amount of your life doing things or acting a certain way because of what others think.

Again, you can be a selfless person and serve others as you choose the direction of your life. Acting authentically and being comfortable to be your true self is not selfish, and when you are comfortable in yourself and make decisions that align with the person you want to become, you will begin to build more authentic relationships, which will lead to making a larger impact on those around you. Sure, you may lose friends along the way and people may say that you've changed, but who says change makes you a bad person? It just proves that they probably didn't get to meet the real you to begin with. Take an inventory of how you act and why you do certain things. Is it because you want to, or is it to fit into a reality that others have carved out for you?

It's scary to be our true self. We fear that we won't be loved as we are, or we doubt that our friends will stick around for the real versions of us. The good news is you know that in moments of self-doubt, you should lean into what love would do. Love would be authentic and trust that the right people will still care about you. Love would realize that it is way better to be who you are with fewer friends than hate yourself for being who everyone else wants you to be. Whether you like it or not, people are going to come and go in your twenties, so ensure that you always have a solid, loving relationship with yourself. This way, as you gain new friends, and old friends fall out of touch, you will always have one relationship you can count on.

Love yourself. Let's gooo!

EXIT HERE | LOVE YOURSELF

Road Map Recap

Engage in the Cycle of Self-Love:

Learn | Understand who you are right now

Accept | Respect where you are in the moment

Decide | Evaluate your options to move forward with this new information

Love | Act in a way that honors your decision

In moments of doubt, choose love. Try your best to love yourself consistently and make decisions that align with who you want to be.

Just be you. Love who you are and don't apologize.

Ask for Directions

How can I love myself in this situation?

Am I acting like my own best friend today?

Add to Your Playlist

Read this book: *High Five Habit* by Mel Robbins

Read this book: *You are a Badass* by Jen Sincero

Pit Stop

Take the free personality assessment here: https://www.16personalities.com/.

Give yourself a high five in the mirror each day for the next 5 days.

FIND YOUR FOCUS
EXIT 2

"You have two choices: You can make a living, or you can design a life."

JIM ROHN

At the end of 2012, P.J. Fleck was hired as the head football coach at Western Michigan University. He took a team that was 1–11 in 2013 to a historical record of 13–1 in 2016. Being from the westside of Michigan, I had loosely followed the story of this high-energy coach and his Row the Boat philosophy, but in 2017 when he was hired by the University of Minnesota, I became infatuated. At the time, I was leading a team of admissions recruiters and I wanted to create the absolute best environment for my team to flourish. I watched everything P.J. Fleck related for weeks looking for any clues of how to replicate what he had done at Western Michigan. YouTube videos, press conferences, game footage—you name it, I watched it. I wanted to learn how to build an elite level culture, and I was convinced that he was on the right track.

One clue that stood out to me was that in P.J. Fleck's Row the Boat culture, there was a unique vocabulary of 217 words. He would give specific meanings to each word, and everyone in the program would have to learn all 217. Some words were simply redefined, but others would be turned into acronyms. For example, he took the word *family* and repurposed it to mean "Forget About Me, I Love You." I loved this idea and got to work on creating acronyms for everyday words in my own life.

This led me to creating the FOCUS philosophy, and it has been guiding my life's GPS ever since. FOCUS stands for Find Opportunities, Create Unique Success. It is a self-growth mantra that pushes me to take advantage of each day and constantly reminds me that I can always choose to be an active participant in designing my future. In times of doubt while I was lacking motivation or direction, I would stop and FOCUS. This has allowed me to center myself and get back on track.

Find | Proactively search for
Opportunities | Situations that align with your vision
Create | Take action
Unique | Special to you
Success | Joy

FIND: PROACTIVELY SEARCH FOR

Ownership is a critical component of the FOCUS philosophy. You have to buy into the idea that you have control of how your life turns out. It's important that you proactively take it upon yourself to search for opportunities to enrich your life and the lives of others. People are willing to help along the way, but you can't expect people to give you anything. As my Uncle Greg often said, "you need to be willing to go out there and take what is yours." You need to be willing to ask for help, and when you feel like you have arrived and there's no possible way you could grow, you need to be teachable and find your next challenge. Your next adventure. Your next level of performance.

To find opportunities, you need enough self-love to chase the things you want rather than sitting back and hoping they happen for you. So look for feedback, seek out connections, and put yourself in a position to be successful. Remember, **you are the driver in this journey, not a passenger.** You have permission to find the roads you want to travel. It's a slight shift in perspective but makes a world of difference in where you end up.

OPPORTUNITIES: SITUATIONS THAT ALIGN WITH YOUR VISION

To become a peak performer, it is imperative to have a sense of where we want to end up. In a general sense, I refer to this direction as your vision. The more clear you can make your vision, the easier it becomes to see situations, circumstances, and people that connect with that vision. For example, if your vision is to lose ten pounds in two months, then you gain immediate clarity on what opportunities you need to take advantage of to turn that vision into a reality. You now see that things like going to the gym and investing in a personal trainer are opportunities. Eating healthy, homemade lunches instead of going through the fast-food also becomes an opportunity. To me, these potential actions are opportunities when your vision is clear. Working out is simply a situation. By itself, working out inherently is neutral. Whether or not it is an *opportunity* is dependent on your vision and what you want in life. This is where you need to love yourself and get real about what *your* vision is. Remember, if you lack vision or clarity on what you want for *yourself*, then you will spend years unhappy as you float through life without a purpose.

Take some time here to do some self-exploration. What do *you* enjoy doing? What lights *your* fire? Where are *you* most passionate? Answering these questions can help you get clear on where you want to go in life. The best part is, once you know where you are going and you have your vision, it becomes a lot easier to identify opportunities! Create your vision, honor your authenticity, and let the search begin!

CREATE: TAKE ACTION

Opportunities have the potential to be powerful, but without action you will never see a difference in outcomes. Become a person who defaults to taking action and makes the most of their opportunities. If you want your life to change, you have to change things in your life. The only way to create movement is through action. I love the word *create* to inspire action because it implies ownership. Again, it is up to you to act and create your reality.

I encourage you to take one small action step at a time. Don't freeze because a task seems daunting or because you don't know how it may end up. Just take the first step, and that action will bring you more clarity. As I coach new business owners who are finding themselves stuck, I have discovered that it's often because they are letting future what-ifs stop them from taking action well within their control. They want to start working with clients but worry what will happen if it goes well, and then they get overwhelmed. They are ready to coach a couple of people but know they are not ready to bring it to a larger scale. This is when I remind them that something is always better than nothing, and to act. In their case, it is enrolling their first client, but for you it might be tackling that to-do list at work, making the prospecting call, or writing up that report for your boss. The big takeaway here is to avoid the negative spiral of what-ifs and simply act. Do what is possible in that moment and keep in tune with your feelings as things progress.

UNIQUE: SPECIAL TO YOU

Throughout our childhoods, we are taught that we are special and unique, but in our teens it is common to trade in our uniqueness to ensure that we fit in. We make compromises along the way to avoid awkwardness or conflict, and we lose sight of who we are. Wake up, start owning your uniqueness, and follow the path that calls you! Motivational speaker, Les Brown, said, "All of us are born unique but most of us die copies."[1] The reason this is true is because people fail to honor their uniqueness in their twenties and become unfulfilled copies in their thirties and beyond. **You are already an amazing person. You are already enough right now.** Remember that.

Listen to yourself and respectfully stay on course. No need to put anyone down, but don't conform just because your current friends or family members don't see the world the same way you see it. You can love them and still chase your own dreams. We can busy ourselves with things to do and lie to ourselves about a path we are on, but it is impossible to enjoy the grind until we are doing something we care about. I think this is why people, especially recent graduates, struggle to find their passion. Through countless conversations with college students and graduates, I would argue that the vast majority of them know what they want to dive into. However, it is rare to find someone willing to take complete ownership of that pursuit. Most people know what they want but worry what their parents and friends will think, or they fear they might fail at the thing they love or that it won't make enough money. Instead of following their unique vision, they start in a career that doesn't allow them to live in alignment. In doing so, they give up their chance to enjoy the grind because they are spending time on things that don't rev their engine. If you feel like I am talking to you, then I want you to know it's not too late live in alignment, but you have to decide to honor your vision.

The sooner you follow your unique ideas and insights, the sooner you can find happiness and ensure you won't die a copy.

SUCCESS: JOY

As you have already gathered, success to me is joy. When you are filled with joy and you are happy more than you are not happy, you are successful. I realize some people measure success in other ways, such as titles, promotions, money, or even influence, but I would argue that if you can consistently be happy, you will reach peak performance and attract those other things into your life. The only difference is that you won't *need* them to be successful. It's truly a win-win, and that is why joy is the final point of the FOCUS philosophy. If you can create happiness in your life, then promotions, titles, and money will follow.

I mentioned this before but it bears repeating: **Happiness is a skill that can be learned.** Just like you can build muscles by working out in a gym, you can practice disciplines that lead to feeling joy. My old definition of success was rooted in promotions, salary raises, and my reputation. And as I accomplished many of these goals, I found that the feeling of accomplishment was short lived. The reason why joy has become my gauge for success is because it ensures that I am checking in with how I feel and making the absolute most of my time on earth. The FOCUS philosophy has led me to many joys. From seemingly small accomplishments like holding a ten-second handstand or breaking forty on the golf course, to life-altering things like losing thirty pounds, starting my own business, and making a cross-country move. The best part about it is that it is a never-ending mantra. When you reach a plateau, it challenges you to find the next opportunity and take action!

Implementing these eighteen disciplines has taken me years, and the FOCUS philosophy has been the glue that held each discipline together. When you have mastered one discipline, stop and FOCUS on what could be next for you and begin the process over again. Each time will strengthen your commitment to yourself and the commitment to continual self-discovery!

Throughout your twenties, it is important to develop your own personal philosophy—your own Row the Boat mantra or FOCUS philosophy. When you have a personal philosophy, you have clarity on where you are going and what it will take to get there. As you ride along the highway of happiness, you will start to naturally develop your own, but I want you to start thinking about it now. Just like P.J.'s philosophy inspired me to create FOCUS, I hope FOCUS will assist you on your trip.

Find your focus and chase your highest potential!

EXIT HERE | FIND YOUR FOCUS

Road Map Recap

Focus: Find Opportunities, Create Unique Success.

You are the driver on this journey, not a passenger.

Create your vision and find situations that align with that vision.

Act. Small actions over time make a big difference.

Listen to yourself. Honor your unique ideas and insights.

Enjoy the process.

Ask for Directions

What vision do I have for my life? Am I following it?

Am I taking action toward the life I want to have?

What is one thing I can do today that aligns with my vision?

Add to Your Playlist

Read this book: *Row The Boat* by Jon Gordon and P.J. Fleck

Watch this YouTube video: "Success is the continual unfolding of the design of our life [Jim Rohn Motivation]"

Pit Stop

Write down your vision for the next two months of your life. Be specific.

Write down three opportunities that would bring your vision to life. These are the steps you can take to achieve that vision. Take action on one of those opportunities today. Create your own reality.

CHOOSE JOY
EXIT 3

> "The last of human freedoms: to choose one's attitude in any given set of circumstances, to choose one's own way."
>
> VIKTOR FRANKL

As you look to be happy amid the personal and professional grind of your twenties, it is important to define what you are after in the first place. The dictionary defines *joy* as, "a feeling of great pleasure and happiness."[1] Following the rabbit hole a bit, I then looked up *happiness*, which is defined as "the state of being happy."[2] These definitions had me running in surface-level circles all day, so I wanted to find a definition that could serve me and my clients. While there are a lot of theories and ideologies out there, I have found deep truth in the definition provided by the former chief business officer for Google X and author of the book *Solve for Happy*, Mo Gawdat. Mo's definition is that happiness and joy can be solved using the following equation:[3]

Happiness ≥ Events of your life - Your expectation of how life should be

Let's dig into my experience as a one-on-one performance coach to bring Mo's equation to life. While I work with predominantly young professionals, I always carve out a few client spaces for college students. Let's lean in and see what we all can learn from a couple of college kids.

HAPPINESS IN ACTION

Seth and Sally walk into class for their final exam of the semester. Seth has attended every class, studied consistently for four hours a week leading up to the exam and has received a 90% or higher on all prior tests in the class. Because of this information, Seth has his heart set on getting a 95% on the final exam (Seth's expectation). Sally, on the other hand, has missed a couple of classes. She is a decent student, but only studies for this class an average of one hour a week and has an average score of 82% on all previous tests. Based on this information, she is hoping to get an 80% (Sally's expectation). They both take their test and try their best. When their tests come back, they both receive a 90% on the final exam (event in life).

Seth is furious with himself. He is disappointed that he didn't reach his goal of 95%. Meanwhile, Sally is ecstatic. She is so excited about her grade and happy to share the news with her parents and friends. The life event is the same. They both received a grade of 90%, yet our friends Seth and Sally are experiencing two very different emotional responses.

This story is directly based on the experience I had while coaching two real people. I had coaching sessions with Seth to work through his disappointment and frustration, and I also got to share in the excitement of Sally getting her first 90% of the semester. This example is real, and it happens every day in school, business, and life.

This is what excites me the most about Mo's happiness equation. *It's a choice.* Yes, to be very clear, it's my opinion and there is a lot of data and research done by people way smarter than me to suggest that *happiness is 100% a choice.* This doesn't mean that we can all choose to be happy twenty-four hours a day, seven days a week or that we would even want to choose happiness all the time, but I do hope it empowers you to realize **you are in control of your emotional state and you can be an active participant in how you feel in response to the things that happen to you.**

If joy is the feeling we get when we receive more than we expect, then we can focus our attention on avoiding a disparity between our expectations and how our life events unfold. Anytime where life doesn't stack up to our expectations, we experience emotional states such as disappointment, fear, regret, and anger. If we want to experience those feelings less, then we simply need to change our perspective on how we set expectations. Setting our expectations is subjective and completely within our control. We are in the driver's seat. When we understand this and accept the reality of it, we can make adjustments to our expectations and feel joy more consistently.

EFFORT VS. OUTCOMES | THE EXPECTATION SWEET SPOT

I know what you are thinking, *Wait, Joe, so you're telling me to lower my expectations? I have always been taught to have super high expectations for myself, so this makes no sense. How can I be a high performer with low expectations?*

Don't worry, you can still be wildly ambitious and happy. I encourage you to continue to set an extremely high bar for yourself while setting yourself up to experience more joy. I believe expectations can be separated into two categories.

Efforts and outcomes. When we manage these expectations properly, we can maximize results and minimize the potential gap between our expectations and life events.

JOE'S DICTIONARY

Effort Expectations: How much effort you *put* into the achievement of a goal. Effort is 100% in your control. You can always expect the absolute maximum personal effort from yourself.

Outcome Expectations: What you expect to come from the effort you put into the achievement of a goal. Outcome is not 100% in your control. You cannot confidently predict all outcomes.

My advice is to consider the outcome you want to achieve and work backward. What type of effort would you need to put forth to achieve such a result? Once you have a clear understanding of the effort needed, focus all your attention on the *effort*. Let go of the need to achieve the result, and place your expectations on executing the effort side of the scale. Because effort is in our control, it is more likely that we can hit the mark when it comes to meeting those expectations. It also places more emphasis on the work, or the grind. The more we are present in the grind, the more we can enjoy the process!

In the story of Seth and Sally, Seth demonstrates a very high level of effort but never celebrates it along the way. He goes to every class and studies diligently; however, he never stops to enjoy the process because he is fixated on the grade he might receive. If his expectations are centered around his effort, then he will be able to feel joy as he goes to class and heads to the library to study. Because we are spending the majority of the time preparing for life's events, it makes sense to allow that to be the time we choose to experience joy. A typical semester is fifteen weeks, and most college classes have four major tests.

Three tests and then a final exam. With this in mind, the daily effort of going to class, and the hours of studying make up 101 of the 105 total days in that semester. That's 96 percent of the semester. The four tests only account for four of the days, or a mere 4 percent of the semester. So my question is, why do we spend so much time obsessed with the result and strip ourselves of so much potential joy in the process?

The outcomes are going to come and go, but setting your expectations in relation to your effort will allow you to focus on what is in your control and worry less about what is not. You will be able to spend most of your time focused on your effort in the present moment rather than stressing about potential outcomes that may or may not happen in the future.

HOW TO CHOOSE HAPPINESS EVERY TIME

It's important to acknowledge that some life events happen independent of our effort. Difficult things will happen to you in your twenties, so I want to equip you with a tool to utilize in any scenario. When your boss adds another project on your plate, when a good friend stabs you in the back, or when a loved one passes away, you need to be ready. Ready to accept what is happening, respect how you feel, and work through your emotions in a healthy way. In a YouTube podcast, Mo referred to a question workflow that he uses to find happiness. It has worked wonders for me and my clients.

Mo's Happiness Workflow

1. **Is it true?** If yes, what can I do about it? If no, you can choose joy.
2. **Can I do anything about it?** If yes, take action and choose joy. If no, move to question three.
3. **Can I accept it and move on despite it being true and out of my control?** If yes, you are choosing joy. If

no, you are choosing fear, sadness, frustration, or anger.[4]

The idea here is not to disregard our feelings and suppress how we feel. The idea is to use the workflow questions to experience our feelings and choose joy in a healthy and efficient way. Sure there are things that are harder to work through and will take longer, but the more you use a workflow like this and rely on the rest of the disciplines in this book, the more time you will be able to spend in a state of happiness. The beauty of a workflow is that it allows us to come to a choice. When we choose a path, we accept accountability for the direction we are taking and give ourselves more control and ownership. The more we feel in control of our life, the more motivated we feel, which leads to happiness!

MAKE TIME FOR JOY

The final element of choosing joy is doing things you like. This one sounds like a no-brainer, but it often gets overlooked. The grind of your twenties is a constant balancing act of school, work, and relationships, so it gets very easy to forget to make time for yourself. If you are going from work to night classes to folding laundry to drinks out with friends, there is very little time for you and the simple pleasures you enjoy.

I challenge you to block time each week for a couple things that you enjoy. For example, I know that I enjoy golfing. I know what to expect when I golf and I enjoy that experience. Because my expectations are met or exceeded when I golf, I always have a good time. Same thing when I go for a walk outdoors in nature. I know what I am getting and my expectations are met or exceeded. Because the formula to happiness is this simple, we need to build in specific time to take advantage of these guaranteed experiences. I realize that we can't all golf twenty-four seven or spend all of our time in the woods, but we *can* carve out time for a few fifteen-minute walks and a trip to the golf course consistently.

Potential Roadblock | Stress from Driving Too Fast

I often refer to life as the race to nowhere. Everyone is racing around, trying to get as much done as they can to make as much money as they can as fast as they possibly can. It's no surprise that everyone is so stressed out all the time, this rush to nowhere is exhausting stuff. In fact, according to Wrike's United States stress statistics from 2019, 94% of American workers report experiencing stress at their workplace.[5] The roadblock here is the timeline that people associate with these ambitions. It's the balance between persistence and patience. The persistence to chase your ambitions is not the cause of all this stress. The persistence is healthy; the persistence is good. The fact you want it all now is what is stifling your momentum and riddling you with unproductive stress. My suggestion: just slow down. Take a breath once in a while and respect that you have a lot of great years ahead of you. You can be persistent in your effort and patient with the outcomes. When you can slow down and remove some of these rushed expectations off your shoulders, you can alleviate all the stress and negative self-talk that is keeping you from actually doing the things necessary to chase those ambitions in the first place.

I want you to have everything you desire in your life. I want you to become the best version of yourself, earn what you are worth, and provide abundance for yourself and others. But to achieve all of those things, *and experience them fully*, you need to be happy along the way.

WHAT IS STRESS ANYWAY?

The Mental Health Foundation of the United Kingdom defines stress as the feeling of being overwhelmed or unable to cope with mental or emotional pressure.[6] In full transparency, I have nothing against stress. Stress is actually a really good thing in moderation and when it is caused by outside factors. In situations where we are in actual danger, stress can be lifesaving. We just have to remember that in the modern world, we are fortunate enough to rarely be in real danger. The days of living in flight-or-fight mode are thankfully behind us, but we spend a lot of our time manufacturing our own pressure and unrealistic expectations. The problem with this is that our brain can't tell the difference between actual danger and perceived danger. These situations are so powerful that it releases the same chemicals and hormones either way. There is very little difference in how our body reacts to actual danger, such as a car accident, and manufactured danger, like trying to make a six-figure salary and be promoted within six months of starting with a new employer. To navigate this roadblock, you are going to have to evaluate where your stress is coming from. Identify what is within your control and what time-sensitive pressures you are trying to live up to. Reframing those expectations will do you a world of good.

You can be the driving force in removing self-imposed stress. While you can't eliminate stress completely, you can become more patient and focus on your effort. This will give you the power to significantly reduce the amount of stress you experience and allow you to better handle stress as it arises.

Take the wheel, slow down, and choose joy.

EXIT HERE | CHOOSE JOY

Road Map Recap

You have the power to choose joy in any situation. Life events will happen to you, but you can be in control of your emotional state.

Set your effort expectations high so you can be an ambitious high performer. Let go of outcome expectations so you can experience more joy.

Making time for activities that you enjoy provides energy to sustain you through the grind of everyday life.

Slowing down and being patient can free us from unproductive, self-imposed stress.

Ask for Directions

Am I proactively choosing joy?
Am I focused on my effort or on the outcome?
Where am I creating stress in my own life?

Add to Your Playlist

Read this book: *Solve for Happy* by Mo Gawdat
Read this book: *A Mind At Home With Itself* by Byron Katie
Watch this YouTube video: "The Happiness Expert That Made 51 Million People Happier: Mo Gawdat | E101"

Pit Stop

Block at least one hour total in your calendar every week to do things you enjoy.

ALWAYS BE TEACHABLE
EXIT 4

"We can know only that we know nothing. And that is the highest degree of human wisdom."

LEO TOLSTORY

When I was working in higher education, I had the opportunity to hire our staff of student tour guides. I would conduct in-depth interviews, and I was constantly searching for people who were easy to talk to and connect with. At the time, I thought the ability to connect with others was the most important skill a new hire could possess. I hired a fair share of charismatic people, but some of them lacked discipline. They would miss shifts or forget about events, so I shifted gears. I needed people to show up, so I began to look for people who were, above all else, disciplined and responsible. I would much rather have someone that shows up than someone who is great with people but isn't there to do the job. Over time, I became obsessed with finding what made the "best" hire. *Surely story-*

telling ability is important, I thought. *No wait, they have to be willing to make mistakes, but they have to have a high attention to detail too!*

As I made the transition from my days hiring staff as an administrator to accepting clients as a performance coach, I found myself saying the same thing. *What am I looking for in my ideal clients? Who specifically do I want to work with and what traits do they possess?* I then began to look outside of my teams and personal connections and listened to people I respected in the business world. My search led me to a ton of consistent results.

Tom Bilyeu lives by a life mantra of ABL, which means Always Be Learning.

Jim Rohn spoke often about being a student of your own life.

Gary Vaynerchuk encourages people to stay curious and say yes to new ventures.

The common message from all these happy and successful people is to avoid becoming stuck in your ways and be open to new ways of doing things. **In other words, the most important trait that any person can possess is the willingness to be teachable.** All the other traits are nice, and I would love to have them as icing on the cake, but nothing matters as much as a person's willingness to be teachable. This one discipline affords you the opportunity to master all other disciplines. If you are teachable, then you are receptive to new ways of doing things, which can impact everything else. For example, if you have a poor attitude but you are teachable, then I can teach you how to be more positive. If you are great with people but frequently are running late, that's fine as long as you are teachable and willing to learn how to be on time. We all have things we are naturally good at and enjoy, and we all have things that we dislike and don't gravitate toward. I am not suggesting that you have to spend your life doing things you don't like, but I do highly recommend that you be willing to learn skills and disciplines that serve you. Doing so will help you improve your strengths and navigate your current weaknesses.

THE TEACHABILITY INDEX

Now that we know it's really beneficial to be teachable, I want to get clear on what it *means* to be teachable so you can start operating through this lens right away. To further elaborate, I want to introduce you to the self-evaluation tool known as the teachability index, as discussed by Kevin Trudeau in the YouTube series, "Your Wish Is Your Command." Trudeau defines a person's teachability index as the sum percentage of the following two variables:

1. Your willingness to learn
2. Your willingness to accept change

Get your teachability score by evaluating yourself on each variable on a zero to ten scale and then multiplying those numbers together to get your teachability index at that very moment of your life.[1] For example, if your willingness to learn is an eight out of ten, and your willingness to accept change is a two out of ten, then your teachability index would only be 16%.

As you are exposed to the disciplines in this book, you should make a conscious effort toward having your teachability index above 70%. I have found that anything above 70% has allowed me to challenge my fixed mindset and make adjustments to my daily routine.

By our twenties, it is natural to feel apprehension toward implementing new things because of our love for comfort. As we learn new things, we understand their benefits but fear pain and sacrifice that may accompany its implementation. The habit of staying comfortable is what keeps us repeating the same patterns, whether they are serving us or not. Keeping our teachability index above 70% lets us be open to making the necessary changes for positive growth. The process of asking yourself a question with numerical answers enables you to turn your subjective feelings into something more objective. Rather than being lost in your head, using the teachability index lets you quickly assess how teachable you are in that moment and how you could act next.

The reason why being teachable while reading this book is so important is that these disciplines will require you to try things outside of your current comfort zone. From activities like journaling and meditation to mindset shifts and philosophies; I am sure you will encounter disciplines in this book that you haven't tried. I want you to look at these as opportunities to grow, and the best way to do so is to approach them with an open mind, ready to learn.

Potential Roadblocks | Knowing It All and Fear of Change

If we want to be teachable, we first have to admit that we don't know everything. As Leo Tolstoy points out, wisdom only comes from respecting what we don't know.[2] The first roadblock you need to avoid is thinking that you know something. As soon as you have convinced yourself that you know something, you immediately become unwilling to learn, which makes you unteachable. This can take some time, but if you get in the habit of questioning what you claim to know, then you will begin to see the infinite depth of knowledge out there. If you can admit that you never truly know anything, then you can consistently score an eight or nine out of ten for your willingness to learn.

The second roadblock we can encounter is in relation to our willingness to accept change. By your early twenties, you have developed a fairly regular daily operating procedure. Your habits and routines got you through college well enough, so you are going to hesitate to accept changes to that routine. The fact is, some of the habits that served you in college likely won't provide happiness and success as you navigate your career. The time of all-night study sessions, classes starting at 10:00 a.m., and no homework on Fridays are replaced with the nine-to-five workday and forty-to-sixty-hour work weeks. You have a foundation, yes, but to ensure peak performance, you need to evolve as your responsibilities and schedule changes. Listen up, because this is important. You are growing up and part of the grind is adapting to a more consistent workload and higher levels of pressure. You can enjoy life more if you grow into the person that can handle the additional responsibilities and commitments, but you will need to act differently to do so. We can reinvent ourselves every day, but we have to be willing to replace old habits for new ones.

YOGA IS FOR GIRLS . . . OR SO I THOUGHT

I attribute much of my happiness to always being teachable and have so many examples of how that has allowed me to change as necessary to evolve into the person I want to be. My favorite example is how I discovered yoga. For years, I had a fixed mindset that yoga was for girls and it was boring, and stupid. (Forgive my younger self.) In those days, my teachability index in relation to yoga was an absolute 0%. I didn't want to learn about it, and I sure as hell didn't want to make any changes to my life to do it. Then, my good friend Bryan exposed me to the concept of the teachability index. A couple weeks later, while reading *The Happiness Project*, by Gretchen Rubin, I was reintroduced to the concept of yoga. I read a couple paragraphs about how yoga was proven to lead to happiness, and thought, *Hmmm . . . seems like yoga might be worth a try after all.* Boom, I let go of my preconceived (and totally incorrect) gender biases and my willingness to learn became a ten. I did a little research and found the right yoga video series for me and committed myself to doing it every day for thirty days. Bam! My willingness to accept change was also a ten. With my index at 100%, I built ten minutes of yoga into my routine, set high effort expectations for myself, and felt extraordinary results. Yoga has been part of my life ever since.

CONNECT WITH CONTENT

> "A reader lives a thousand lives before he dies. The man who never reads lives only once."
>
> GEORGE R.R. MARTIN

A big piece to becoming teachable is surrounding yourself with people and material that will expand your mind. Today we have access to so much inspirational and thought-provoking content, and it's your job to build it into your daily routine. Whether you grab a book to read, listen to audiobooks, or watch podcasts, immerse yourself with content that stretches your way of thinking. Learning from other people's journeys will save you time and enable you to get the most out of life!

I prefer to listen to audiobooks while I follow along and make notes in the hard copy of the book. As someone with dyslexia, this strategy has dramatically supported my retention of what I am listening to, but I realize it's not for everyone. It doesn't matter how you connect, as much as it matters that you are carving out time to do it. This exposes you to new content, which triggers new ideas, which leads to action!

To tackle the disciplines in this book, I had to be highly teachable, meaning I had to be receptive to learning *and* willing to implement it in my life. Trust me when I say this: don't wait until you're twenty-eight to really lean into making changes.

The changes are worth it, the journey is amazing, so just do it now. Expose yourself to new ideas and accept the change that needs to happen so that you can become your happiest self.

Be teachable!

EXIT HERE | ALWAYS BE TEACHABLE

Road Map Recap

Being teachable allows us to receive and implement new ideas, habits, and disciplines quickly.

The teachability index is the product of the following two variables:

1. Your willingness to learn (0–10 scale)
2. Your willingness to accept change (0–10 scale)

A teachable mindset is what creates a rich environment for shifts in your identity.

Be intentional about connecting with new ideas. Read, watch, or listen to something new every day!

Ask for Directions

What is my teachability index right now?

Add to Your Playlist

Read this book: *Happiness Project* by Gretchen Rubin

Listen to this YouTube series: "Your Wish Is Your Command" by Kevin Trudeau

Pit Stop

Choose one specific point of tension in your life right now and apply the teachability index to identify what is holding you back!

WORK FOR FUTURE YOU
EXIT 5

"What I find most amazing about pro athletes is what they are willing not to do. What they're willing not to eat, what they're willing not to say."

TREVOR MOAWAD

It was my third week as a door-to-door salesperson and I just had back-to-back days without sales. Having one hundred people tell me no was fine, but having no sales in between to soften the blow was rough. On the outside I didn't let it show, but I was rattled. I had just left my nine-year career in college enrollment and moved my entire life to North Carolina to run my coaching business full time. I was fortunate enough to have a friend who owned his own pest control company in the area, and he was willing to let me sell door to door to help make ends meet. The problem was that I would only be making financial ends meet if I was making sales. For the past two days, I had just been walking around neighborhoods collecting nos, and I was starting to doubt myself.

It's always hot at the end of August in North Carolina, but when it's ninety degrees and you haven't made a sale, you start to think of all the things you would rather do. I wanted to go golfing and binge-watch Netflix in the air conditioning with my wife. I started to say negative things out loud like *I can't do this* or *what am I doing here?* Lucky for me, I was surrounded by a great team of leaders. I was encouraged to keep knocking and to rise to the challenge. As Trevor Moawad points out, peak performers are willing to make short-term sacrifices for long-term results.[1] For me this meant being willing not to say negative things out loud. It means focusing on the opportunity in front of me and giving up golf and Netflix for a couple of months.

Through this process of self-evaluation, I was reminded of a discipline I had adopted years ago: to work for your future self. Sure, I had a couple hard days and my ego had suffered a blow, but what I was most afraid of was the work. I didn't want to go back to the doors because the days are long and being told no was frustrating. The simple fact was that if I put in the work now and knocked doors consistently, then I would make the sales, and in the future, I would have a steady stream of income for the next few months. I remembered that my action and sacrifice today on the doors would result in my future ease and comfort. I went to work for Future Me the next day with a renewed sense of purpose and energy. I ended up hitting seventy-five sales part-time in three months, which secured Future Joe and Future Keisha a free cruise to the Bahamas!

SACRIFICE

Congratulations, you just got hired for the most important job of your life. No, I am not talking about your current job, or working with your current team, or organization. I am talking about the most influential job you have in your life and the person you will work for well beyond the end of your professional career. You guessed it, it's you!

The next few years of your life are going to be full of sacrifices. If you want to excel in your career, you will have to sacrifice time out with friends. If you want to grow as an individual, you will have to sacrifice time away from loved ones staying late at the office in order to read and reflect on your own. The list of sacrifices goes on and on. The trick is to be aware of sacrifice and be intentional with the sacrifices you are making. Make sure that the sacrifices align with your vision and understand they are short term. The seasons of your twenties will ebb and flow, and your priorities will change. If you can adapt the mindset that you are constantly working for the future version of yourself, you can immediately build a strong positive relationship with sacrifice. It helps you associate positive intention with the actions and efforts that are required to experience more joy and enhanced performance.

Sacrifice comes in two forms: sacrificing for other people and sacrificing for ourselves. Because this journey is about how to find joy within yourself, it's critical that you understand the difference between the two.

Sacrificing for Others

Throughout our lives, we make a positive association between being selfless and its contributions to the people we care about. We study on the weekends because our parents are helping pay for school. We run extra sprints to be in shape for the team, or we practice late so we can contribute to the rest of the pep band. We sacrifice our time or short-term feelings, with the justification that we are giving up what we want to contribute to a greater purpose and future happiness. I see endless value in making sacrifices for other people because it creates trust and a deeper sense of connection. These relationships that we build create a sense of duty to others, which can be quite motivating and enhancing to our lives. Making sacrifices for others on my teams, in my relationships, or for organizations definitely leads to better results and more happiness throughout the journey.

Sacrifice for Yourself

The other opportunity is to make sacrifices for ourselves. When I talk to groups or coach my clients, I often introduce the idea of the Future You, which supports the idea of seeing yourself as your own best friend. It is easier to sacrifice for your future self because you can conceptualize and imagine your future self as someone separate from your current self. I came across this concept in my early twenties in relation to long-term saving. A study had been done where people were shown a rendered image of themselves at age sixty-five. The participants were then asked a series of questions in relation to their daily spending. Participants that had been shown the picture of their future self were far more likely to save their money and invest in their retirement than the participants in the control group who had not seen the image of their future self. By seeing a photo of an older version of themselves, the participants in the study became more aware of the reality of aging. This heightened awareness of their future self caused them to act differently in the present to create a better future. They were willing to make sacrifices now to invest and save because they could clearly see the impact it would have on them when they were sixty-five.

The concept of Future Me made sense, so I started applying it to short-term things as well. Current Joe didn't want to work out today, but Future Joe wanted to be fit come summertime, so Current Joe went to the gym. Current Joe didn't want to make fifty cold calls to recruit students, but Future Joe wanted to hit his recruitment goal at the end of the year, so Current Joe picked up the phone.

We have to realize that the emotions we experience now are temporary. Joy or sadness, excitement or doubt, they will all pass. Using this to our advantage, we can build in the discipline to think about our future selves and how we will experience more positive emotional states in the future if we make a sacrifice for them now. When I first started to act in accordance with Future Me in mind, it was a way to trick myself into going to the gym or putting in the extra time at work. Over the years, working for my future self has created a relationship of self-love. This is why it is so powerful to reframe the why behind what you are doing. No matter what company you work for, what team of people you work with, or what outside goals you are given, you will be able to maximize your personal growth and happiness when you take ownership and take action because it will benefit Future You. If you adopt a mindset that only works for a boss, company, or organization, then you give yourself an out when it comes to ownership and accountability. When you work with Future You in mind, you create a habit of taking extreme personal ownership, which we know leads to freedom and happiness. Reframing who you work for allows you to bring more purpose to the tasks on your to-do list, which can be a powerful motivator and eventual reward.

The hard truth is that happiness and success are on the other side of sacrifice. In his book, *Can't Hurt Me*, David Goggins says, "I found true happiness on the other side of suffering."[2] That can be difficult to hear, but we don't have to resist the struggle. If you work for Future You, then you give purpose to your struggle. It's still a grind, but we get to enjoy it rather than resent it. Rather than feeling burdened or frustrated, you can get excited to endure the challenge because of the positive impact it will have on your happiness and mental health!

There is a great quote by Les Brown:

"If you do what is easy, your life will be hard. If you do what is hard, your life will be easy."[3]

In my life I have found this to be extremely true, but it can be difficult to implement. To help me stay motivated and persistent, I have applied the concept of Future Joe to the mix. If I want Future Joe's life to be easy, I need to do difficult things today. The hard thing now will always lead to more joy later, so as you start to explore this discipline of working for the future version of yourself, I want you to redefine *hard* tasks. Working for our future selves helps us practice looking beyond the short-term difficulties in our lives and connects those difficulties with the benefits that come from the fruits of our labor. When we see the powerful impact of the effort we put out today, then it allows us to be happier in the present moment and enjoy the grind.

Get to work for yourself, and you will thank yourself later!

EXIT HERE | WORK FOR FUTURE YOU

Road Map Recap

All emotions are temporary, so be willing to sacrifice short-term emotions for long-term happiness.

Working for Future You strengthens your relationship with yourself and allows you to see the personal benefits of your current efforts.

Ask for Directions

How will my actions today impact my life tomorrow?
Who am I working for right now?

Add to Your Playlist

Read this book: *It Takes What it Takes* by Trevor Moawad with Andy Staples

Read this book: *Can't Hurt Me* by David Goggins

Pit Stop

Do one thing today to help Future You be happier tomorrow.

PART TWO
ROUTINES

MASTER MOTIVATION
EXIT 6

> "You can motivate by fear, and you can motivate by reward. But both those methods are only temporary. The only lasting thing is self-motivation."
>
> — HOMER RICE

As I speak to more groups and provide impromptu coaching to strangers, I find one of the most common roadblocks people face is a lack of motivation. People want to be happier and perform at the next level, and in most cases, they already know what they need to do. The obstacle is finding the motivation to actually do it. If this is you and you are struggling to find motivation, I want to start off by saying it's not your fault. Society and formal education have done a great job of depicting motivation as something you have or you don't have, so it's really easy to get down on yourself when you are lacking motivation. We feel like some people have it and some people don't, and we are rarely taught how to create healthy motivation for ourselves. The truth is, we all have times in life when we don't feel like doing something. Peak performers accept this fact and find a way to stay motivated despite how they are feeling in the moment. During your visit in this exit, I want to give you some rationale as to why you may feel a lack of motivation in your twenties and some guidance on how you can create your own moving forward!

WHERE DID IT ALL GO?

Motivation is just like happiness in the sense that it is a skill to be mastered. The more ownership we take and intention we give to motivation, the more it will show up for us. The problem is that throughout high school and college, we have an abundant amount of outside motivators. We are predominantly motivated by grades, social status, team involvement, and living up to other people's expectations. Life events also play a role in motivation. As our childhood takes shape, we become motivated by how events impact our lives and the feelings we associate with those events. This is all very natural, but inherently, it doesn't allow us to build the skill of creating our own motivation. We become dependent on outside motivation.

Now that you are in your twenties, you have a much stronger sense of independence. The years that shaped you were critical, but you may be finding that some of those external motivators are producing less results. This is okay. Just like tread on our tires, certain motivational factors lose traction over time. It's important to begin replacing old external motivators with more self-serving, intrinsically driven factors. The bottom line is you are in the habit of being motivated by outside factors that no longer motivate you. It's not your fault, but you do need to do something about it. You need to become an expert self-motivator.

THREE-WORD PHRASES

During my time at Adrian College, I had the privilege of working with Chris Cook. He is one of the most routine and disciplined guys I have ever met. A true high performer. One day we were hanging out and he mentioned a motivational phrase that one of his old high school coaches taught him. His coach would tell Chris and his teammates to wake up swinging, that life was a fight and you had to wake up every day with your arms swinging, ready to fight the day. From the first second I heard this, I adopted it as my own. Despite being constantly exhausted, I had recently been promoted, so I was trying to wake up and get into the office earlier. I started using the phrase to get my tired ass out of bed. This mindset helped me attack the day and create the energy and motivation to get up and get going. It gave me a way to look at my morning and instantly find purpose and control.

I was astonished how one simple phrase could lead to so much intrinsic motivation. What I realized was that the three words were clear enough to remember quickly, but vague enough to create deeper, more motivating intentions. The more committed I became saying my phrase out loud, the more successful I became in executing and taking aligned action. I would also write it on sticky notes and put it places I would see it, like next to my bed or on my bathroom mirror. Because I was laser focused on improving my morning routine, it was the perfect phrase for me at the time.

After a couple of months, "wake up swinging" had become a regular part of my vocabulary and routine, so I figured it was time to craft my next phrase. I have found that one new phrase every month is a motivational sweet spot. It's a long enough time period to commit to the phrase but it's short enough that you don't become bored of it.

CREATE YOUR OWN MOTIVATIONAL PHRASE

Creating your own three-word phrase is powerful because it ensures connection to the meaning and motivation behind the phrase. In moments when you lack motivation, you will have an automatic go-to phrase that you created and feel strongly about. Here is my formula to come up with meaningful and motivational phrases for you:

1. **Look Ahead** | See what is on your calendar for the upcoming month. What are you looking to accomplish? What projects will you have at work? What will you spend your time doing?
2. **Identify Your Identity** | Ask yourself, who do I want to be this month? How do I want to show up? What energy do I want to bring?
3. **Brainstorm** | Think out loud and list what comes up for you after you have reflected on the first two questions. I typically just say them out loud, but a lot of my clients write out a list of options.
4. **Choose and Consolidate** | This is where you pick the direction you want to go and shorten it into only three words. This process is challenging but powerful. In moments of lack, you need to be able to quickly remember your phrase, so limiting the phrase to only three words is key!

Not only does a three-word phrase serve as a call to action and quick motivator, but it puts into simple terms the identity we are seeking to become. Wake up swinging, says "I am a morning person who attacks the day." Setting a new phrase every month allows us to shift our identity gradually over time. Your phrase will serve as a constant reminder of who you want to become and the journey you are on to get there. Positive and encouraging self-talk has also been linked to intrinsic motivation and high performance, so make sure to say your phrase out loud and put it where you can see it. Print it out, write it down, or save it on your phone's lock screen, whatever works best! When you feel the feeling of stepping away from action, or taking the easy road, just say your three-word phrase and act!

BONUS MOTIVATION TOOLS

Because motivation is such a hot topic, I wanted to equip you with a few more motivational tools or concepts. I hope some of these help you create more motivation along your drive.

The Five Second Rule. Author and coach, Mel Robbins, brought the entire world a game-changing technique when she wrote and shared her book *The Five Second Rule*. The premise of the rule is simple. When you don't feel like taking action throughout the day, just count down from five and then *move*. What started out as a way to get herself out of bed in the morning, ended up having a tremendous impact on how people see motivation and can overcome inaction. After further research, Mel found that the Five Second Rule is a form of meta-cognition, which basically allows you to trick your brain into action before it has enough time to keep you from doing things that you don't feel like doing. I cannot recommend this book enough, but if you don't take time to read the book, please take the time to implement the rule.

As someone with ADHD, the Five Second Rule is a tool that I use frequently throughout the day to keep me on task and to overcome moments where motivation is nowhere to be found. As I notice myself drifting to social media sites rather than doing my work, I will go "5-4-3-2-1" and close out of Facebook or Instagram. When I don't feel like working out, I count "5-4-3-2-1" and press play on a yoga video. It's a strategy that anyone can implement. You are a five-second decision away from peak performance!

Pack a Lunch. As I mentioned, we are all motivated by people, ideas, and experiences. Having a physical reminder of these things to see and touch can be very motivating. A couple of years ago, I decided to intentionally collect some small items that represent people and concepts that motivated me, and then put them in a metal lunch box. Just to name a few, some of the items are as follows: a small Rubik's cube to remind me to be a problem solver, a stack of poker chips to motivate me to take calculated risks, a toy police officer badge to remind me of friendship and sacrifice. They are all small in size, but they represent deeply impactful ideals. When I am feeling tired, or lazy, I grab my lunch box because I know it always brings me inspiration. The old school metal lunch box reminds me to "pack a lunch" and get to work, and it has become the home to many motivational tokens that I have acquired through the years.

During the self-editing phase of this book, I began to doubt myself and started to lose motivation. Rather than giving up, I grabbed one item from my motivational lunch box as I started to edit and re-write each chapter. Each item was a reminder of a person, experience, or blessing that I had in my life, and it provided me with the perspective to push through. In the moment, I didn't have the motivation to finish the book, but thankfully, years ago, I decided to collect motivation for when I would need it. My lunch box gave me what I needed to finish this book and has helped me through many challenging times.

You don't need to use a lunch box, but I strongly suggest you create a go-to well of motivational tokens. Find a container, shelf, or space that has significance to you, and start to put small motivational keepsakes in it. They could be items or even pictures—whatever has significance to you. This way, when motivation is low, you know where to go!

Star of Your Own Show. Imagine you are starring in your own Netflix original documentary, and a camera crew is following you around to document your every move. How would you act? What would you do with your time? And how would you respond if you were being filmed all day, every day? The camera crew is looking to film you to find out what it is that makes you a success, so you better not disappoint!

I used this a ton while working from home and growing my coaching business on social media. It motivated me to avoid distractions and kept me on task.

Schedule in Motivation. If you use a planner or calendar, then take a few minutes to add motivational reminders at random times throughout the year. You could use put motivating quotes in your planner, leave reminders to Future You from Current You, or even ponder life-altering scenarios to bring you perspective. For example, I have a random reminder in my calendar that says, *imagine you are diagnosed with a terminal illness*. It pops up on my calendar every four to six months, and it motivates the hell out of me. I realize this might be a bit morbid, but remembering that our time on earth is limited can be very motivating.

Assume the Best. Often, we become demotivated because we assume the worst as we plan. We *want* the best, but then our mind immediately assumes our plan won't work, we won't get the help we need, or we won't be able to bring the idea to life. After a couple minutes, we completely talked ourselves out of taking action. These assumptions lower our motivation levels, stifle progress, and don't serve us. Flip the script and make assumptions work for you by assuming the absolute best. Assume you will have the time, get the support, and crush it. This will raise your excitement level and increase your chances of getting started!

Invest in What Works. With all these self-motivation strategies, I am hopeful you have found something that helps you; however, I do want to point out that self-awareness really matters when it comes to motivation. If you still can't create consistent intrinsic motivation, then invest in consistent external motivation. Maybe you just prefer having someone else to be accountable to, and that is okay! Don't spend your life wishing you were able to motivate yourself, just accept it and seek the support you find motivating. Hire a life coach, personal trainer, or at least ask a friend to hold you accountable to your goals. Whatever it is, make the time to create the opportunity to be motivated on a consistent basis.

Be sure to fill your tank with the motivational fuel you need to be your best!

EXIT HERE | MASTER MOTIVATION

Road Map Recap

We can't wait for motivation to show up for us. We need to create it in our lives.

Our priorities and what we find motivating changes as we age. Don't get discouraged if you are no longer motivated by the same things.

Setting your own motivational three-word phrase is a powerful tool. It's short enough to remember and vague enough to provide depth of purpose.

Find what works for you and stay consistent. Discipline and consistency will always compensate for low motivation.

Ask for Directions

Am I creating my own motivation or waiting to be motivated?

What bonus motivation tool can I implement now?

Add to Your Playlist

Read this book: *The Five Second Rule* by Mel Robbins

Pit Stop

Create your own three-word phrase for this month!

The more you say and share your phrase, the more you will become accountable to it. Post about your three-word phrase and what it means to you on Instagram and tag me! @joevangeison

WIN THE DAY
EXIT 7

"Problems that are procrastinated are only amplified, and we are the ones that pay the price."

RORY VADEN

As an admissions counselor, I learned that high school students struggle with focusing on the step immediately in front of them. Instead of submitting their college applications to their top schools, they were thinking two steps ahead and already worrying about the financial commitment. Their fear associated with the cost led to procrastination and kept them from taking the first step in the process. To combat this fear, I built into my presentation to them a question that I had heard from famous football coach Lou Holtz. The question was, "What's important now?" I loved asking this question because it had the acronym of WIN.

Being a competitive person and someone who likes to win, I would start my presentation to high school students and say, "Today we are going to WIN. Today we are going to answer the most important question that we can, which is, What's important now?" This would allow the students to see that completing their college application essays or scheduling a campus visit were most important now, and they could tackle the harder tasks once they had completed the first steps. This allowed them to get started rather than procrastinate. Once you identify what is most important, you can focus all your attention and energy on that task. The clarity will allow you to be more effective and can also leave time at the end of the day to take care of less important or less urgent things.

LET'S ALL WIN

As you level up in your career and beyond, you will constantly be challenged by how to spend your time. You will be forced to make countless decisions on what matters and what doesn't, so make sure to use this simple question as often as you need right away. You will start off using it consciously, but as time goes on, you will naturally find yourself evaluating situations by using WIN as your filter. The power behind this question is the *now* part of it. Deciding what's important *now* allows you to rank things based on a level of importance *and* urgency. When you come to your answer, it becomes much easier to manage your time, and you'll feel less stressed in the process.

SET A TIMER AND COMPETE

Now that you know what to do, you still must do it, so here is a quick trick to take action and avoid procrastination. Time itself can be a great motivator, so setting timers for specific activities can allow us to use time to our advantage. When we lack structure, it is easier to waste time, or give below-average effort toward the task at hand.

Setting a timer while we work allows us to pour energy into

that task because we have an end in sight. For example, doing the dishes or folding the laundry can be tedious tasks that can drag on for far too long if we don't set expectations around the action. Setting a five-minute timer to unload the dishwasher or setting a ten-minute timer to fold the laundry can create a sense of urgency that gives us a reason to work through the task at an effective pace and just get it over with.

Setting a timer for tasks also gives us a clear understanding for how long they take. When you know that loading and unloading the dishwasher only takes five minutes, it makes it easier to do it now rather than blow it out of proportion and procrastinate. Sometimes you will finish ahead of the time allotted, and sometimes you will realize you need more time to complete something, but either way, just the act of setting the timer is practicing your newfound respect for time. Time is our most valuable asset, so it's important we treat it as such. You can apply this to literally every task that you have in front of you, so set a timer and get to work!

Make It a Game | You vs. The Clock

Setting timers can capitalize on our internal drive to compete. I realize that some people are less competitive than others, but at a core level, most people like to see progress. Exploit this by making a game out of the things on your to-do list. If you have six tasks to get through by the end of the day, set a fifteen-minute timer and rotate the tasks every time the alarm goes off until they are complete! This allows you to focus solely on the completion of one task and limit distractions.

Setting timers is also a strategy I use to break down larger tasks. For example, if you have an entry-level sales position, you may need to make two hundred cold calls by the end of the week. Two hundred calls is daunting, and to be fair, not very exciting. Getting hung up on, being told no, and leaving voicemails can get redundant quickly. Picking up that phone to make the first of two hundred calls can be stressful, so we may avoid it, which will only leave us feeling more overwhelmed later that day. Setting a timer to make calls for thirty minutes, seems way more manageable! Anyone can make calls for thirty minutes and no matter how overwhelmed you feel about the goal, the first action of calling for thirty minutes is well within reach. A successful, young salesperson is going to be someone who can break up their time into small blocks solely focused on calling, rather than stressing over the end goal of making the two hundred calls. (See Exit 9 for more about breaking up large projects into smaller tasks.)

The great part is that this strategy works for literally every facet of your life. Set a timer for chores around the house, projects at work, going for walks, meditation, whatever! I used time blocks and setting timers to write this book. After some trial and error, I found that sixty-to-ninety-minute timers would lead to the best results of focused attention and writing flow, which brought me clarity on how I could realistically complete the project.

Commit to a Calendar

Now that you have a practical way to identify tasks worth working on, you need a place to put them. Consider each task and event and assess how long it will take you to complete them. The benefit of putting your to-do list into a calendar is that you can see where your time will be spent on any given day. Without a live calendar, it becomes very easy to let minutes, hours, and even weeks pass by. The best way to avoid this is to put important meetings, commitments, and tasks on your calendar ahead of time so you can plan accordingly. We are so lucky today that our online calendar connects with our phones and we can constantly update it and make changes. When something is important but you don't have time for it today, create a calendar event for later in the week. The process of planning ahead will also allow you to stress less and focus more on enjoying the present moment!

Focus on the Good. Another benefit of using a calendar is the positive feedback loop it creates. As a young professional trying to climb the ladder, you are going to run into moments of self-doubt. You are going to wonder if you are doing enough to impress your boss or be a good co-worker. Rather than wonder, you can look back at your calendar and get real-time feedback. If you have empty days where you didn't contribute, then you know there is an opportunity to produce more. If you see a streak of five straight days of being productive at work, getting to the gym, and a few occasions where you made time for friends, then you can be proud of all that you are accomplishing!

The Oil of Life. As we have discussed, building a loving relationship with yourself is imperative. Using a calendar is a tangible way for you to show up and forge that relationship. The calendar holds you accountable to yourself, which is a massive form of self-love. It also establishes a bond with Future You. As you set plans for the future, you are ensuring that Current You is taking care of business for Future You. As you implement the disciplines in this book, you will need a system to rely on. You will need oil to keep your engine running smoothly, so commit to a calendar and start making the time for your personal development. Build in time for your weekly reflections and block off time for your morning routine, evening practice, and to connect with your community.

As a young professional, you will be bombarded with things to do. Emails to answer, clients to respond to, calls to make, and errands to run. I don't want you to *manage* your time, I want you to lead yourself into taking deliberate action. The emphasis now becomes what to do and where to put your energy. Jim Rohn used to say, "don't major in minor things,"[1] and the earlier you can determine what is major and what is minor, the sooner you will take off in your career and enjoy the process. The art of making decisions and deciding what you will and won't spend your time on is a skill. Having a go-to question like *What's important now?* and using a calendar to organize your days can allow you to deliberately practice the skill more frequently, which allows you to refine the skill faster.

EXIT HERE | WIN THE DAY

Road Map Recap

Asking yourself, *What's important now?* allows you to rank things based on a level of importance and urgency.

Set a timer and get to work!

A calendar is a powerful and practical tool that you can use as you implement new disciplines in your life.

Ask for Directions

What's important now?

Where can I start to use a timer in my life and work?

Do I currently have a live digital calendar? If not, why not?

Add to Your Playlist

Read this book: *Deep Work* by Cal Newport

Pit Stop

Use a timer three times this week to race the clock for tasks you need motivation for (chores, answering emails, etc.).

Commit to using a live calendar. Take fifteen minutes on Sunday night to plan out your week in advance, try your best to stick to your commitments, add and move tasks as you go.

HANG THE LIGHTS
EXIT 8

"Big things are accomplished only through the perfection of minor details."

JOHN WOODEN

When I was twenty-three years old, I was a volunteer assistant hockey coach at Adrian College. Late in the season, there was a scheduling conflict and our normal head coach was not able to attend a game. This was my chance. My head coaching debut! Truth be told, we were playing the last place team in the league, and our players could have won without a coach that night, but I didn't care. I was so excited to deliver the pre-game speech. This was my big break to inspire the team. The best part was that no one was expecting it. With an interim head coach and a lackluster opponent, our guys were ready to take care of business, but they didn't expect anything from me.

It's easy to motivate people when it's a big opponent because their adrenaline is already pumping, but the true challenge is inspiring people to take on the mundane. I whole-heartedly accepted that challenge. After hours of running through my speech by myself in the car, I got to the rink. I practiced it a couple more times while the team was stretching and getting dressed, and then I went in, as if I were Mike Babcock himself, and delivered this gem:

Gentleman, when I was driving back to campus today, I passed a house with a woman outside hanging her Christmas lights. She was on a rickety ladder, struggling to hang the lights around a large pine tree in her front yard. I could tell she was fatigued and frustrated, but nonetheless, she was on the top of that ladder, hanging those lights. I got to thinking, you hardly ever notice people hanging their lights. You never remember the struggle and commitment it takes to get them up, but when that first snowfall comes and the darkness of night sets in, their house becomes the visual representation of the beauty and the magic of Christmas. And then it's worth it.

Now, boys, we are more talented than this team, and we will win this game, but when you hit the ice tonight, I challenge you to hang the lights. Tonight is an opportunity to do the little things right. It's nights like these where no one will acknowledge that you are backchecking, or staying positive on the bench, or that we are executing the refined nuances of our systems. But when we get to the national tournament, when our backs are against the wall, when that first snow fall comes and the darkness sets in, we will revert back to the disciplines that we reinforce tonight. And there will be magic, and we will be champions.

Now let's go hang the lights.

The team hung the lights that night with a focus on perfecting the little things. We won the game with a 10–2 victory. Later that year, we advanced to the national tournament and would go on to win the ACHA DIII National Championship. We would be fortunate enough to win it again the next two seasons, completing a three-peat. What a privilege that was to be part of such a special time of Adrian College hockey history. I connected with so many amazing people in those years, and although I was a coach, I know they taught me a hell of a lot more than I ever taught them. The guys on those teams showed me what it means to hang the lights, and they showed me the profound impact that paying attention to the details can have. They also taught me about the balance between discipline and fun. To perform at a high level, you have to commit to excelling at the little things, but they also let themselves have fun on and off the ice. Their celebrations were an early glimpse at the possibility of enjoying the grind. They proved that you *can* have both.

As you begin to navigate your years after college, make sure to hang the lights in your life. Just like that woman in the story, you are going to get tired and frustrated with tedious tasks, like answering emails, managing your calendar, staying organized. At times, you will be overworked and underappreciated, but push through and hang your lights. Don't worry about getting credit or acknowledgment, just hang your lights. I promise you, doing the little things day in and day out will lead to more moments of joy than you can ever imagine.

Hang the lights and make every day feel like Christmas!

EXIT HERE | HANG THE LIGHTS

Road Map Recap

Anyone can get excited by the big moments in life, but peak performers find joy in even the most mundane tasks.

Executing small tasks to the best of our abilities allows us to be present, which allows us to be happy.

Give yourself validation for completing day-to-day tasks rather than expecting others to notice and validate your actions.

Ask for Directions

Am I taking care of the little things behind the scenes?

What little things can I get done today?

Add to Your Playlist

Read this book: *Leave No Doubt* by Mike Babcock

Pit Stop

Create a list of mundane but important tasks in your life. Whether it's emails for work or keeping up with the laundry, get it on the list! Add these tasks to your weekly calendar to ensure that you are making the time to get them done.

LOOK FOR LAY-UPS
EXIT 9

"A little bit of something beats a lot of nothing. Break the largest of difficult tasks into the smallest of steps and it can be done."

DAN MILLMAN

In basketball, a lay-up is the easiest shot to make. You are as close as you can be to the basket, and you are far more likely to make a lay-up than a mid-range jump shot or a deep three-pointer. By now you may have realized that life likes to present us with more three-pointers and half-court shots than lay-ups. You find yourself juggling big projects at work and lofty goals in your personal life, leaving you uncertain if you can even make the shots. Happy high performers can take on big challenges because they have developed the skill of breaking big shots into smaller, more manageable lay-ups. They look for lay-ups within the larger task that will create the momentum they need to eventually accomplish the big stuff. The other critical component of a lay-up is that you have to take the ball to the hoop. You can't sit back and wait for a pass and then shoot. You must drive the lane on your own.

For some more realistic examples of looking for lay-ups, let's check in on a few of my clients. In our weekly coaching sessions, I help them plan out their ideal week so they can execute at the highest level possible. As we craft the week, it becomes evident how people default to taking on more than they can chew. They put the big things on their to-do list like bill fifty hours by Friday, submit a graduate school application by the end of the month, or plan an entire trip to Hawaii in four days. This is a fine starting point to set the vision of where we want to go, but again, these are three-pointers and half-court shots. We want lay-ups, and lots of them. Lay-ups are the small effort based tasks that will eventually produce the end result we are looking for.

LOOKING FOR LAY-UPS IN ACTION

Let's use the example of trying to plan a trip to Hawaii. There is so much associated with that one task that the thought of starting the process can freeze anyone. So let's look for lay-ups, easy wins we know we can handle. Here are a few that come to mind immediately.

- Review the calendar and discuss potential dates for the trip with my spouse.
- Spend thirty minutes researching flights.
- Share flight information with my spouse and book the flight we want.
- (x2) Spend thirty minutes researching possible hotel and rental car options.
- Discuss options with spouse, then book hotel and secure rental car.

- (x2) Spend thirty minutes researching excursions we can go on.
- Discuss options with spouse, then secure excursions and activities.
- Spend thirty minutes getting familiar with our hotel location and its accommodations.

Planning a trip like this will take a couple weeks at least, so breaking down the big task into smaller fifteen-to-thirty-minute-long action steps can allow us to systematically build momentum, which will keep us engaged and encourage us to keep going!

Believe it or not, some of us get in the habit of putting easy tasks to the side. We figure the job is easy and it will only take a couple minutes, so we put it off.

THE MAGIC OF MOMENTUM

In his book, *The Talent Code,* author Dan Coyle, discovers that the world's best performers chunk things down.[1] From a scientific point of view, our brain is built to accomplish small tasks until mastery, which leads to more mastery. When we chunk down our skills and work on them deliberately, myelin forms around the nerves of the brain, reinforcing what we are doing and helping us execute at a higher level. We see similar findings in James Clear's book, *Atomic Habits.* Clear encourages us to break down large goals into super easy and manageable tasks to create habits that stick.

When trying to develop a new habit, he recommends starting with two minutes or less of action. Want to become a pianist? According to Clear, you should play the piano for two minutes early on in the learning curve. Want to lose 100 pounds? Start by going to the gym for just two minutes on a consistent basis. These concepts sound simple, but they both capitalize on the power of momentum. This is why looking for lay-ups is such a beneficial discipline to master.

If you spend your time taking manageable action, you are doing two important things for progress. First, you are making progress so you will feel like doing more. If you have completed multiple small steps, you are far more likely to feel engaged in the process and persist to completion. Second, your brain is literally developing a default to action. Because you are intentionally taking action over and over again, your brain is getting practice being a starter rather than a procrastinator.

As I have mentioned, a common roadblock for my clients is overcoming procrastination. The ambitious and driven young professionals that I work with have big dreams, which often means big gaps in daily execution. While it is critical to have a big vision for what your life can entail, sometimes a big dream seems too far out of reach. Their initial motivation quickly switches to procrastination when they realize their goal or dream is years away from coming to fruition. This is where combining disciplines can become helpful. For example, once you have identified what's important now, you can break that down into lay-ups and take action. This allows you to get started on the right things and tackle the large task one piece at time!

If you haven't noticed by now, a very common theme on this road to happiness is action, and this discipline is no exception. The art of looking for lay-ups in your life helps you break things down into easy steps, but you must drive the lane and take care of business. A lot of people struggle to do life's simple tasks. Ironically, we find it hard to do easy things. Looking for lay-ups will help you break your big tasks into manageable activities, but you it's still up to you to act.

Break down your jump shots into lay-ups and get to work!

EXIT HERE | LOOK FOR LAY-UPS

Road Map Recap

Looking for lay-ups is the process of breaking down large, stressful tasks into small, easy-to-handle steps.

Completing small tasks consistently builds momentum, which encourages further action.

Ask for Directions

What tasks, goals, or responsibilities do I need to get done?

How can I break them down into more manageable action steps?

Add to Your Playlist

Read this book: *The Talent Code* by Daniel Coyle
Read this book: *Atomic Habits* by James Clear

Pit Stop

Choose one thing you've been putting off and break it down into manageable steps. Write down these steps and do one at a time until the entire task is done.

RISE AND GRIND
EXIT 10

> "Early to bed and early to rise makes a man healthy, wealthy, and wise."
>
> BENJAMIN FRANKLIN

In 2020, our oldest dog, Maggie, had her first seizure. It's hard to describe how difficult it is to watch a dog have a seizure, but what I can tell you is that if you witness it once, you will do everything in your power to avoid it ever happening again. For us, this meant that Keisha and I would have to take turns waking up at 4:30 a.m. to give Maggie medication that helped prevent her seizures. It was not ideal waking up at 4:30 a.m., but when it keeps your dog from having a seizure, you make it work. Today, Maggie only needs medication twice a day, and we have adjusted her schedule to later in the morning, but in the years of waking up at 4:30 a.m., I learned a lot about waking up and the science of sleep. Keisha and I shared the responsibility of giving Maggie her medication, but on my mornings, I started staying up at 4:30 a.m. and working on my coaching business until 7:30 a.m. I dove into the science of sleep, habit formation, and motivation to understand what allows people to wake up early and perform at their best. I took bits and pieces from sleep physiologists, authors, and coaches and developed a system of tools that helped me maximize my sleep efficiency, which dramatically impacted my mood and my performance. I refer to it as my Peak Performance Foundation, and it can help anyone improve their sleep habits.

PEAK PERFORMANCE FOUNDATION

In my experience, sleep tends to be the first thing we overlook when we consider performance and the first thing we sacrifice when we run short on time. Sure, it worked in college when we had to pull all-nighters to finish our midterms and final projects, but those days are over. *Remember, you are in the driver's seat!* It is time to get serious about creating a sleep schedule that works for you and the lifestyle you want to have.

The Peak Performance Foundation is created through the mastery of three phases of your day: your first five minutes, your morning routine, and your evening practice.

YOUR FIRST FIVE

Giving Maggie her medication helped me realize something that I think is very important to share. Waking up at 4:30 a.m. was just as frustrating as getting up at 8:00 a.m. Whether you sleep in until noon or wake up around 5:00 a.m., you are still met with the same frustration as you get out of your warm, comfortable bed. If you wake up with a great attitude every day, then more power to you, but I never have. My first emotion, every morning without fail, is anger. Waking up for Maggie helped me see that either way, you aren't going to feel like getting out of bed, so you might as well get out of bed earlier, choose to have a good attitude despite those feelings and attack the day.

Once you accept the fact that the first few minutes will be difficult, you can create a plan to help you during your time of need. This plan is the habit loop that you want to go through to ensure a great start to your day. Because you are aware of the motivational power of a three-word phrase and the five second rule from Mel Robbins covered in Exit 6, I always recommend you start there. You wake up and likely feel anger and frustration. That's okay because you knew it was coming. Now, you immediately make the choice to think of your three-word phrase and then count down from five. As soon as you get to zero, you get out of bed. By this point you are up, and it's only a few seconds into your morning.

This is where you can pick an additional two to four quick actions that help you start things off right. For a full list of options and ideas, make sure to visit my website, but here are a couple things to consider doing in the first five minutes. Make your bed, brush your teeth, stretch, give yourself a high five in the mirror, or drink some water. All super quick and proven to kick start your day!

POTENTIAL ROADBLOCK | HITTING THE SNOOZE BUTTON

If you have trouble hitting the snooze button, then I have great news! It is just a habit that you have adopted over time. Hitting the snooze button is just proof that you can create habits in your life. The challenge now is to replace your habit of hitting the snooze button with positive habits that allow you to take control of your day within the first five minutes. Creating your own first five will allow you to avoid the snooze button and start the day with some immediate wins! Let's gooo!

A MORNING ROUTINE FULL OF OPTIONS

As someone who works with people on forming new habits, I have noticed that momentum is critical to consistency. We try something new for a couple days and we feel great, but life can happen to make us lose momentum. Our intentions are great, but we easily get thrown off by interruptions to our routine. This could be getting sick for a few days or having to travel out of town for work, but we want to ensure that these hiccups don't prevent us from becoming a peak performer. This is why I recommend people design three morning routines so they are ready for whatever life throws their way. Here are the three different routines you can proactively create to ensure you are in control and staying on track!

Max Morning: This is your ideal morning routine. This should include everything you would want to do if you woke up on time and were feeling great. You have maximum time and energy, so take advantage. Get a full workout in, shower, do your hair, meditate, read, journal, get to work early, go for a run, you name it! Do all the things that fill your tank with no need to rush!

Quick Morning: For a variety of reasons, there will be days that you oversleep your alarm or simply do not have enough time to go through your max morning routine. It's important on these days that you have a plan so you can still execute and make continued progress. Maybe you are traveling and don't have the normal amount of time that you have at home, or maybe you don't have access to your home gym. Whatever the reason, having an adjusted plan ahead of time lets us still feel success and enjoy the benefits of momentum as we shift our sleep-morning habits. If you normally work out for thirty minutes and then journal for fifteen minutes, consider doing a five-minute stretch and five-minute journal reflection instead.

Lower the time or the number of activities in a way that still has you feeling great!

Lax Morning: This is when you are feeling under the weather or overly tired. It's okay to rest. Part of enjoying the grind is stepping away and resting from time to time! This routine is meant to allow you to relax and ease into your day. It could include a walk instead of a run, or a stretch instead of a workout, and it's also great for weekends, when you are looking for something restorative.

Having options as you level up your morning routine lets you respect your body while continuing to win. Rather than feeling like you have let yourself down if you don't have time for your max morning, you can feel the win of executing your quick morning instead. In the first couple weeks, you should strive to have one to two max mornings, while executing your quick routine or lax routine on the other five to six days. Over time, keeping the commitment to ourselves by executing one of the three routines leads to that stronger relationship with ourselves and makes us more likely to continue with the shift in identity rather than the short-term attempt to just wake up earlier. In week three and four, you can push for executing your max morning routine three to four times a week. A peak performer typically finds a good flow of five max mornings, one quick morning, and one lax morning per week. Obviously, you can adjust if you are sick or depending on the season of life you are in, but building up to five max mornings a week can have a profound impact on your mood and output!

YOUR EVENING PRACTICE | THE SLEEP SECRET NO ONE IS TALKING ABOUT

I have a secret for you. It's likely the most overlooked fact of sleep. A secret so simple that you have missed it or disregarded it.

The absolute key to waking up earlier . . .
Here it is . . .
Go to bed earlier on a consistent basis.

I know. It's a radical concept, but it's true. If you go to bed at the same time and it's around 10:00 p.m., then you can get awesome, restful, joy-filled sleep and wake up feeling great. If you already go to bed around 9:30 p.m. or 10:00 p.m., then I am sorry for being so sarcastic, but if you are still going to bed at midnight or 1:00 a.m., then this section is for you.

I want you to really pay attention to what you are doing from 10:00 p.m. to bedtime. I realize that there is a very small percentage of people who perform meaningful work late at night, but the vast majority of my clients realize that they are wasting the hours of 10:00 p.m. to 1:00 a.m. For most of them, it isn't intentional. It is just something they have become accustomed to because it's how they functioned in college. Now is time to hit the reset button, so start paying attention to when you are going to bed and what you are doing before bed. Just because you *can* stay up late watching TV, playing video games, or catching up on emails or social media doesn't mean we *should*. This is not my opinion; it's completely based in science and how our bodies function.[1]

As you raise your awareness of the subject of sleep, I highly encourage you to dive in further by reading *Sleep Smarter* by Shawn Stevenson. His research-based strategies to getting better sleep have done wonders for me and my clients. Here are some immediate tips and takeaways from his book that will hopefully help you reconsider how you approach sleep and when you go to bed.[2]

- Head to bed around 10:00 p.m. when your body is naturally winding down.
- Sleep in ninety-minute intervals to wake up feeling rested. For example, if you go to bed at 10:30 p.m.,

then you should wake up at 6:00 a.m. That will give you five 90-minute cycles of sleep, and you will wake up feeling rested and energized.
- Go to bed within thirty minutes of the same time each night and wake up at the same time each day. Even on the weekends!
- Make your bedroom a sleep sanctuary. Remove TVs and other distractions, and use blackout blinds to get it as dark as possible for optimal rest.

I want you to be happy and enjoy the day, and sleep plays a huge role in our mood and how we handle our emotions. Sleep deprivation takes a serious toll on how we process information and navigate difficulties, so put yourself in a position to be successful when it comes to your sleep. The best way to do this is committing yourself to an evening practice. It's super easy, and it will give you purpose as you head to bed.

First, you need to set your bedtime. Put it in your calendar, tell your spouse or roommates about it, and stay committed to it. Once you have a consistent bedtime, pick two to three actions that you will do before bed. Some suggestions would be to set out your clothes for the next day, pack your lunch, brush your teeth, or read. All these options will help you get away from screens and wind down and feel prepared for the next day. It's that simple!

NOT A MORNING PERSON, NOT A PROBLEM!

These days I consistently wake up between 6:00 a.m. and 6:30 a.m., but I want to be very clear that I was not always a morning person and I am not always perfect. Keisha will be the first to tell you that I dislike getting up, and I still do hit the snooze button from time to time. (She really hates when I sleep through my alarm because it wakes the dogs up and interrupts her sleep, so I promise she will tell you!)

That said, the impact that good sleep has in our lives is undeniable and you can do something about it. You may not be a "morning person" now, but that is just a label that you have given yourself. Pay attention to how you approach sleep, take the time to create your own peak performance foundation, and give yourself a new label.

Rise and grind. You got this!

EXIT HERE | RISE AND GRIND

Road Map Recap

Sleep is very important to happiness and performance, but it is often overlooked.

Create your own Peak Performance Foundation by taking control of your first five minutes, your morning routine, and your evening practice.

Sleep in ninety-minute increments. This allows you to wake up at the end of a sleep cycle, making you far more likely to wake up feeling rested and energized! (This means 6 hours, 7.5 hours, or 9 hours of sleep per night.)

Ask for Directions

Am I sleeping in ninety-minute increments?

If I stay up past 10 p.m., what am I doing with that time? Is it worth it?

Add to Your Playlist

Read this book: *Sleep Smarter* by Shawn Stevenson

Pit Stop

Create a morning routine for your first five minutes.

Create a plan for your max, quick, and lax morning.

Create an evening plan to help you wind down and prepare for the next day.

Access My Peak Performance Sleep Tracker Here: bit.ly/enjoy-the-grind.

RESPECT YOUR BODY
EXIT 11

"Eat like you love yourself. Move like you love yourself. Speak like you love yourself. Act like you love yourself."

TARA STILES

One of my favorite things about being married to a first-grade teacher is the stories I get to hear when my wife gets home. Kids in general are funny, but first graders are at the age where they are really coming into their own, which leads to some awesome "aha" moments and, oftentimes, amusing realizations. While the students provide most of my amusement normally, on this particular day, it was Keisha.

Keisha entered the house on an absolute mission. The door opened, she flew by the entryway, down the hallway, through the living room, and into the kitchen counter where I was standing. She threw her bag down, hopped on one foot, and grabbed her other foot with intensity. Keisha ripped off her shoe, held it upside down, and shook it violently. At last, a pebble fell to the ground. She picked it up and held it high in the air as if she were King Arthur displaying Excalibur the moment he pulled the sword from the stone, and proclaimed, "This has been in my shoe ALL day!" Keisha then explained to me how the pebble had snuck into her shoe during morning recess, and she had every intention of getting it out, but the day got away from her. She had to get the class settled from recess, then it was snack time, then time for math, then a student needed help tying their shoe, then Jason pushed Tommy, Nicolas needed to go to the bathroom, and before she knew it, it was the end of the day. This is how life happens though. This is how we can all go full days, weeks, and sometimes years without removing the things from our lives that don't serve us.

So often we allow the hustle and bustle of everyday life to get in the way of super simple acts of self-care that would allow us to feel better and perform at a higher level. As a recent college graduate and new professional, you have a lot going on in your life right now. You started your first job, moved into your first apartment or house, bought a new car, you're managing your own money, and on top of all that, you're trying to balance all of the relationships in your life. Old friends, new coworkers, potential romantic relationships, and on and on and on. It's a lot. And it's easy to forget to allocate time each day for your health and wellness.

Just like Keisha had to manage her busy classroom, I know you have to show up for the demands of your new lifestyle, but for goodness' sake, take a second for yourself and get the pebble out of your shoe! *Right now* is a huge opportunity to make a little time each day to care for yourself so that you set yourself up for success.

I know that you are thinking. *Joe, I have so much on my plate right now, there is no way I have time for myself.* But that is exactly why I am encouraging you to build the habit of self-care now. As we learned in Exit 1, Love Yourself, our relationship with ourselves is the foundation for our relationship with happiness, so before you can be truly effective at work, we need to effectively care for ourselves. I love the quote at the beginning of this Exit by Tara Stiles because it simplifies the complex idea of self-care. This exit will help you to see the mind-body connection that exists within each of us, and how you treat your body can impact your happiness and performance.

MOVE YOUR BODY

I originally wanted to title this section "Hit the Gym" because my tendency over the years as a male is to assume that lifting weights in a gym is the best thing for everyone. However, thanks to remaining teachable, I have found yoga, stretching, and walking to be life-changing endeavors. Just move your freaking body in whatever way you feel is best for you. Again, this takes a loving relationship with yourself to actually do what *you* want instead of what you think others want for you, or what is cool, or what is "normal." Consistent movement over long periods of time will do so much more for your health and wellness than a couple weeks of doing something that you hate so much that you don't stick with it.

I experienced this firsthand a few years ago. After years of being an athlete and going to the gym consistently, I found myself having trouble staying committed to working out. I realized that playing team sports had always been the motivator in my late teens and early twenties, but that season of my life had ended. It was time to reframe my vision for my health and wellness. I had to take accountability for why I was working out in the first place. I needed to work out with Future Me in mind, instead of my teammates or athletic aspirations. Once I was able to clearly define why I wanted to work out, then I could find the proper workout plan for the next season of my life. Another great example of how having a clear vision allows you to see new opportunities!

Gone were the days where I needed to be in playing shape, which was leading to my frustration with the gym. All the work outs were designed to get me in shape to play hockey, and I was no longer playing. The work outs were long, I would constantly get distracted by others in the gym, and at the end of the day, I wasn't seeing any of the fruits of my labor because I wasn't playing hockey. Reading books like *The Happiness Project* and *Ikigai: The Japanese Secret to a Long and Happy Life*, helped me understand that I was less interested in being a hockey player or a bodybuilder and more interested in living a happy and healthy life.

With my new purpose of happiness and longevity, it became easy to trade in my gym membership for a yoga mat. I googled "free yoga for men" and stumbled across a thirty-day men's yoga challenge, offered by DoYou Yoga. The instructor offered a daily yoga flow geared toward men for just ten minutes a day! (Talk about a lay-up! It makes so much sense why I stuck with it.) The videos were short, sweet, and to the point. Difficult enough to challenge me but inspiring enough to keep me coming back for more.

Remember, consistency over time is where we see changes, so this was huge. I was understanding what I enjoyed, and I was honoring myself by showing up. Every time I hit the mat, I was subconsciously saying, *This feels good to me* and *I love myself enough to show up and get that good feeling.* For someone who had been used to putting in subpar effort and long hours at the gym, I didn't expect much from completing the challenge. After all, it was only ten minutes a day. But by the end of the challenge, my mood improved, I developed a stronger mind-body connection, and I was physically more flexible. But most importantly, I had realized that I loved yoga, and I didn't care who knew.

I used to think yoga was for women and the gym was the only place for a guy. (Ha! How wrong I was.) Once I accepted the fact that I enjoy yoga, and I let go of people's expectations of what I did, the world opened up for me.

This inspired me and Keisha to investigate other yoga video programs, and we found a twelve-week fitness challenge. This was a series of weekly yoga videos geared toward women, but my teachability index was 100%, and I was willing to try anything. Keisha and I spent the next few months juggling between the men's thirty-day yoga challenge and the twelve-week women's total body challenge, with frequent walks in between. We stayed consistent and I lost forty pounds. Just doing women's yoga with my wife, and I got one firm butt in the process!

If you hate running, then walk. If you hate walking because it's boring, then try an online interactive dance video. If you aren't motivated to work out by yourself, then join a class or ask a friend to go with you! Health and wellness in your twenties can look and feel however you want, so get creative to stay active. You could swim, bike, hike, do martial arts, paddleboard, kayak, play soccer, the list goes on and on! Whatever it is, stop lying to yourself about what you should be doing because other people do it that way, and honor yourself and your actual fitness goals. With so many at-home workout programs and options available, you have abundant opportunities to feel great physically while staying at home. I have clients on weight loss journeys who have made tremendous strides by heading to the gym, while others simply bike a few times a week and mix in yoga when they can. Whatever it is for you, it's important to pick something and keep moving your body.

Being consistently active is great for your mental health and happiness, so I encourage you to be teachable and try new exercises and activities to keep things fresh and interesting. You may hike in the summers and go to the gym in the winter, but by mixing it up, you are able to be revitalized and active throughout the entire year!

EAT RIGHT FOR YOU

I have always been fascinated with different diet plans, and because of my ADHD and short attention span, I have tried a ton of them. Keep in mind, I have always been a relatively skinny guy, so my interest in dieting wasn't necessarily driven by weight loss, but it came from a place of how to feel and perform my best. Watching Netflix documentaries like *What The Health* and reading books like *Genius Foods*, helped me gravitate toward a more plant-based diet. For about a year, my wife and I went fully vegan. We then adjusted to becoming vegetarian, and then landed on a now infamous self-proclaimed title of being flexitarian.

JOE'S DICTIONARY

Flexitarian: A predominantly plant-based diet with the flexibility to eat meat if it was provided at a family function or potluck-style gathering where everyone had to bring a dish to pass. (I mean who can pass up BBQ meatballs at a Superbowl party or Thanksgiving Turkey at your yearly Friendsgiving gathering? Come on . . .)

Diet Plans

More recently, I have taken an interest in and adopted intermittent fasting, which I have really enjoyed. It fits into my lifestyle, it's simple to stay committed, and for the most part, I get to eat whatever I want within my not-fasting window. Daily intermittent fasting has also allowed me to create a stronger relationship with my body and mind. It's insane to feel and understand what our body can do when our mind is open to it. While I have done some more extreme fasts, I normally try to stick to a 16/8 fasting window. I fast for sixteen hours between

8:30 p.m. at night and 12:30 p.m. the next day, and then I eat in the window of time between 12:30 p.m. and 8:30 p.m. This helps me avoid snacking before bed, it allows me to feel light and energized for morning yoga, and I can still enjoy a good lunch and dinner.

As you read this, you may be thinking, *Wait a minute . . . what about breakfast? Isn't that the most important meal of the day?* (Yup, I've tried that). Or, *Wait a second, I heard that you are supposed to eat six small meals throughout your day to keep your metabolism working to keep you energized.* (Done that one too!) As I mentioned earlier, there is no lack of diet options, and most of them contradict each other so dramatically that it can become a challenge to know which one is "right" and which one is "wrong."

The truth is—or at least what I have found—is that what's right and wrong is different for everyone and will vary throughout different seasons of their lives. My go-to dietitian that I refer all my clients to is a friend of mine named Ellen. She has given me great advice on what foods to be eating, how to keep a healthy pantry, and how to shop effectively, but what I respect about her most is that her philosophy is centered around building a healthy relationship with food.

Throughout your twenties, I encourage you to try different things, spice it up in the kitchen literally and figuratively, and overall, build a strong, loving relationship between your body and the food you eat. The food we consume provides us with the energy we need to attack the challenges in our days, so try your best to give yourself the fuel you deserve. When you come from the space of building a positive relationship with food, then you can naturally cut out some of the foods or eating habits that don't serve you. For example, if we use caffeine or energy drinks as a short-term fix to provide energy, then it's easy to grab a can of Red Bull. When we nourish our bodies with foods that provide sustainable energy throughout the day, it's much easier to cut out the short-term fixes and give up pop and energy drinks.

Your twenties will be filled with shifts in lifestyle and purpose, and you need to make sure that your physical well-being and diet support your lifestyle every step of the way. It can get difficult at times, but it will be worth when it comes to your happiness. Being active is a very healthy way to relieve stress and anxiety, and it keeps you feeling great and more resilient as you face challenges.

Respect your body, and your mind will thank you!

EXIT HERE | RESPECT YOUR BODY

Road Map Recap

Happiness is directly connected to what you consume and how you treat your body.

Make sure to re-evaluate your fitness goals throughout your twenties.

Consistent moderate exercise can have a tremendous positive impact on your physical and mental health.

Be willing to try different diets and fitness plans to find what works best for you!

Ask for Directions

What am I trying to achieve through fitness and diet?

Do my current actions match the vision I have for my future wellness?

Do I eat and drink as if I love my body?

Add to Your Playlist

Read this book: *Ikigai* by Hector Garcia and Francesc Miralles

Read this book: *Genius Foods* by Max Lugavere and Paul Grewal

Watch this Netflix documentary: *What the Health*

Pit Stop

Make a list of five physical activities that interest you right now.

Pick one activity and commit to it regularly for the next thirty days.

REFLECT EVERY WEEK
EXIT 12

"No goals, no growth. No clarity, no change."

BRENDON BURCHARD

"All right, before we get too far into the call, let's go back and reflect on last week." This is how most of my one-on-one coaching calls go with my clients. Everyone wants to get into the current opportunity or discuss what they are looking forward to that week, but it's rare they have taken the time to complete their reflection from the previous week. In our fast-paced world, especially as young adults, we move from week to week without taking the proper time to gain clarity on how the last week went. The greatest teacher you can have is *your immediate past*. You just have to carve out the time to explore it. This is exactly why I have my clients type out a quick reflection before we meet each week. It allows us to discuss and explore together so we can identify opportunities for growth at a faster rate.

Don't get me wrong, being present in the moment is absolutely critical to being happy, but carving out specific time to reflect allows us to live in the present more often. So much of the stress and overwhelm you experience is in relation to worrying about the future or dwelling on the past, so when you make time to reflect on the past and plan for the future, you put your present self back in the driver's seat. Knowing that we have set aside time to reflect and connect with the week allows us to stay more present in the moment, because we know we will have the chance to revisit thoughts and emotions in the future.

When we have a frequent and healthy relationship with our past, it creates a feedback loop that allows for a productive cycle of adjustments and learning. The quote at the start of this Exit is so profound because it concisely explains the cycle of personal growth. Until we get clear on how our experience is going, we cannot change, because we are not aware of what is holding us back. Through consistent weekly reflections, we raise our level of awareness, gain clarity, and it becomes easier to identify opportunities to improve.

I try my best to do my weekly reflection on Sunday night as I am winding down before bed, and I ask the same of my clients. Throughout the years, I have tried a mix of different questions but have found these three to be the most effective:

1. What did you learn?
2. What did you enjoy?
3. What do you want to improve?

These questions are open ended so that you can reflect on whatever comes up for you during that moment. If you do this every week, you will be amazed at the nuances and patterns of life that you notice.

WHAT DID I LEARN?

We learn so much in a week. You can miss it if you don't make the time to reflect. We are constantly learning—learning about ourselves, about others and about the world around us. Tony Robbins once said, "What we focus on determines how we feel. And how we feel—our state of mind—powerfully influences our actions."[1] Throughout the week we learn so much, and we feel an extraordinary amount as well. To me, the power of intentional reflection brings focus to what we learn and how we feel. Without a weekly reflection, that feeling might get lost in the myriad other feelings and experiences of the week. When you sit down on Sunday and think back to all that you learned, you can relive the positive feeling and you get the chance to relearn what afforded you that feeling. By writing out your reflection or typing it, you revisit it in your head and see it for what it is. This focus can allow you to act differently in the future.

My clients and I all frequently find that we are learning some of the same things over and over. For example, a client of mine, let's call him Jack, learned that he would get stressed if his email inbox was over ten emails on Monday morning. Jack felt overwhelmed as soon as he sat down at his desk and would procrastinate most of the morning avoiding emails from the weekend. Jack realized that he felt bad because there was a two-to-three-day delay with his responses to emails he would receive on Fridays and over the weekend. He worried that people were upset about his delayed responses, so he would avoid responding, which obviously led to more stress and unwanted pressure. Once we became aware of what was creating the stress, then we could identify strategies to mitigate these feelings so he could look forward to Mondays rather than dreading them and serve his customers more effectively in the process. He decided to set aside thirty minutes at the end of the workday on Fridays to clear out his email inbox. He also then set an out-of-office automatic response, which let his customers know that he would respond to their emails on Monday when he returned. Because he was clear with his customers with what to expect, he felt better about going in on Monday and responding to emails.

Without a weekly feedback loop, we may miss trends like this in our life and then struggle to implement change—doomed to repeat the same mistakes and deal with the same stressors. Asking yourself, *What did I learn this week,* paired with a high teachability index enables us to dramatically reduce the amount of mistakes we repeat. Ask this question of yourself and you won't spend your entire twenties making the same wrong turns!

WHAT DID I ENJOY?

By this point, you shouldn't be shocked by this question at all. It's an oldie but a goodie, and it helps ensure that our GPS is always pointing toward joy. If you get in the habit of typing out or writing out what you enjoy each week, then you will start to notice patterns. I type my weekly reflections up so that at the end of the year I can copy and paste them into one easy-to-digest year in review. It ends up being fifteen to twenty pages, and I read it like a book. I consider it my personal growth story of that year. It is so helpful to comb through the pages with a highlighter looking for trends. Especially in the joy category. If you are struggling to find your passion or understand what you should do for the rest of your life, just track what makes you happy for fifty-two weeks, and you will have your answer. When you notice patterns, it's easier to make time for those activities and enjoy life.

It's always rewarding for me to see my clients reflect on three to six months of their weekly reflections, especially when it comes to the joy question. Seeing months of joy reflections *always* helps bring perspective to what really matters in our lives. Week by week, you are able to effortlessly identify what is making you happy, without pressure or expectation, which is why I know it can help people find their passions and purpose in life. Rather than having to answer the big question of *What should I do with the rest of my life,* you get to look back and see what you enjoy doing week to week. Then, if you love yourself and are teachable, you can make sure you build those things into your life on purpose.

The cool part here is that we get to experience joy throughout the week, and we get to experience the emotions again when we write our reflection. Hello! Double the joy? Count me in!

Over the years, I have noticed a few major trends in what makes me happy: spending time with Keisha, visiting family, and doing yoga, to name a few. These are no surprise to me, and I likely would have identified these with or without a weekly reflection. But not all trends are as evident, which is why the reflection can be so helpful. One thing I never noticed was how much I loved listening to audiobooks. I started listening to books in my early twenties to pass the time while I was driving, but week after week, year after year, I would reference audiobooks more frequently than anything else. It's crazy that I missed it for so long, but after a while, listening to books became a habit, and I started taking it for granted. That said, I would frequently highlight enjoying clips from books and interacting with new books in my week-to-week reflections. If someone would have asked me what I enjoy doing, I never would have thought that listening to a book or podcasts were so high on my list, but now I know it is a critical element in my happiness equation. Now, I proactively use this information by building in time throughout my day to listen to audiobooks. Truth be told, I just love connecting with ideas, and audiobooks have become my pathway to experience more ideas than I could ever imagine.

Start taking note of what you enjoy from day to day. You may be surprised by the trends you find!

WHAT DO I WANT TO IMPROVE?

This is the FOCUS-related portion of the reflection (See Exit 2). This is where I lean into how I am feeling as I try my best to Find Opportunities to Create Unique Success. With fresh thoughts of what you learned and enjoyed racing through your mind, you are likely to have a desire to improve in relation to what you learned or enjoyed that week. No matter what comes up for you, answering this question allows you to create purpose in your life and take ownership as you plan for your next week. Where there is purpose and ownership, there is motivation and an opportunity for growth. Just imagine for a second if you took five to ten minutes to complete this reflection every week. Think about how much happier, smarter, and effective you would be if you committed yourself every week to improving one skill or discipline. It's exciting, and completely in your control. I know you're busy, but this can be a real game changer, so don't overlook it.

Start a digital journal on your computer, or write it out by hand, I don't really care. Just do it. Take the time to pull off the busy highway for a second and reflect. I promise it will give you clarity on where you want to go next!

EXIT HERE | REFLECT EVERY WEEK

Road Map Recap

Weekly reflections serve as immediate positive feedback loops.

What we focus on, we feel, and what we feel impacts our behavior.

Carving out time to reflect on our past and plan for the future allows us to live more fully in the present.

Ask for Directions

What did I learn?
What did I enjoy?
What do I want to improve?

Add to Your Playlist

Read this book: *The Motivation Manifesto* by Brendon Burchard

Pit Stop

Gain access to your own weekly FOCUS workbook here: bit.ly/enjoy-the-grind.

Grab a journal, spiral-bound notebook, a laptop, sidewalk chalk, anything you can put these questions in and answer the above questions every single week starting this week. Review your journal yearly to find trends.

PART THREE
LIFESTYLE

CELEBRATE SUCCESS
EXIT 13

> "The small wins, the tiny triumphs, the everyday victories . . . celebrate them, they will take you there."
>
> ANONYMOUS

It was a big night at the Van Geison household. I had just launched the Rise and Grind Academy, my first virtual group coaching program, and tonight was our first call. I filled the program with ten people, and I was pumped. I had prepared religiously for the call and brought a ton of energy. I executed on every main point I wanted to make, I created a fun atmosphere, and even had my wife, Keisha, sit in on the call so she could provide me with feedback. The call ended and I basically ran out of my home office to meet Keisha in the kitchen to see what she thought. Then the unexpected happened. I saw her come around the corner into the kitchen and I blurted out,

"Well, that sucked."

She of course immediately said, "Not at all! Joe, it was really good, you nailed it!" Then I told her a couple minor things I could have done differently, and she proceeded to convince me that I did a good job. I was reading *The High Five Habit* at the time, so fortunately I was seeing myself in a new way, and I noticed there was a tension between how I wanted to treat myself and how I was treating myself. I was doing the exact opposite of giving myself a high five in the mirror. I was putting myself down and for no reason.

It makes sense now, looking back. I was nervous, so I started by putting myself down before I received feedback. This way, I protected myself from hearing anything that may have hurt my ego. Throughout my twenties, I had become extremely hard on myself so I didn't appear weak to others. Years of putting myself down had resulted in me defaulting to it, and I hadn't even noticed. I didn't understand that I could strive for excellence and celebrate success all at the same time.

Truth be told, I felt great after that first call of the Rise and Grind Academy. I should have run out of that room and yelled to the hilltops that I did an awesome job and I had a blast doing it. So that's what I do now. I have a mirror right outside my home office and on every group call, one-on-one client call, or project that I make progress on, I look at the mirror and celebrate how I did. This, repeated over time, has created momentum and a willingness to fail, which has helped me overcome so many obstacles and limiting beliefs in my business.

THE BIG, THE SMALL, CELEBRATE IT ALL

Celebrating the small successes along the way gives you energy and the consistency needed to see long-term positive results. And, by the way, it feels great. It allows you to enjoy the process rather than delaying joy until a certain outcome or benchmark is reached. By this point, you are looking for lay-ups, setting timers, and killing your to-do lists, so it's about time you celebrated all that progress. Let's be honest, if you want to be promoted, it will likely happen in your career. It's not really a matter of *if*, it's a matter of *when*. So, rather than working for years to feel one moment of joy, I want you to feel freaking amazing every step of the way!

Celebrating small wins is a great way to build a stronger relationship with yourself because you give yourself positive feedback when you execute at a high level. By frequently celebrating progress, you show yourself that your love is unconditional and is not determined by a result. As long as you are showing up and trying your best, you are worth celebrating!

TURN THAT FROWN UPSIDE DOWN

When I share this idea with people, their first question is *Where do I start? What should I celebrate and how exactly can I do it?* I recommend finding a couple situations that frustrate you at work or around the house—where you feel overly critical or lacking control in the final result. The goal here is to turn your moments of frustration into opportunities for celebration. For example, I was being overly critical at the end of each coaching call, which was leading to frustration and doubt—neither of which were helping me or my clients. Now, I celebrate the things that were in my control, and it makes me excited to hop on the next call.

I know it sounds silly, and somewhat corny, but it works. There is a ton of science that our brain can't tell the difference between when we are happy and when we are acting happy, which creates a real opportunity here. For example, did you know that if you sit up straight and smile, your brain will send signals to the rest of your body to send you a dose of feel-good hormones, such as dopamine and serotonin?[1] If you play your favorite song and dance around the living room, your brain will light up as if it were at a dance party with hundreds of people. I don't typically like using the phrase "fake it until you make it," but in this case, you can literally trick your brain into producing a cocktail of happy hormones just by acting happy. To me, celebrating myself and my small wins throughout the day is how I ensure I am making time to act happy. So, turn that frown upside down and act happy. It will make you happy for real!

CELEBRATION IN ACTION

Celebrating yourself will feel weird at first, so here are a few of my favorite ways to celebrate wins big and small.

- **Create a playlist** of songs that you associate with celebration and happiness. When you do well, intentionally play a song from the playlist and have a quick jam session. Dancing/singing along are not required but highly recommended. (Seriously, when you listen to, *We Are the Champions* by Queen as you celebrate doing a mundane task like the dishes, you'll understand.)
- **High-five that mirror or a friend.** I work alone from home, so I high-five a lot of mirrors, but if you work in an office setting, then give out some high fives to other live humans. I know this sounds weird, but just tell them you like giving out high fives to celebrate small wins. The first time is a little awkward, but after that, people will have no problem joining in.
- **Write out your wins!** Take a minute to celebrate your progress by writing a celebratory journal entry. Jot down all the recent wins you have had and how they made you feel!
- **Say positive things to yourself out loud.** Self-talk is super powerful, so don't be afraid to give yourself a "Let's gooo!" or "Great job" when you execute!

- **Reward yourself.** You won't find deep intrinsic worth through external rewards, but it can be healthy and motivating to celebrate bigger wins. Treat yourself to a nice dinner or new pair of workout shoes when you hit a milestone!

I want to take a moment to remind you that life is whatever you make it. You can choose to be happy or you can choose to be sad. You can choose to make life a race or a joy ride. Whatever you decide, try to make it a celebration!

EXIT HERE | CELEBRATE SUCCESS

Road Map Recap

Take your small wins, or your biggest frustrations and turn them into celebrations.

You can have big goals and ambitions, and still celebrate the small wins along the way. It builds momentum and makes the big wins more likely.

Your posture and body movement can assist you to change your mental state and the emotions you experience.

The more you act happy, the more you will feel happy.

Ask for Directions

How can I celebrate today?

Am I my biggest fan or my biggest critic?

Is my life currently a celebration? If no, what will I do about it?

Add to Your Playlist

Listen to this song: "Celebration," Kool and the Gang

Listen to this song: "We Are the Champions," Queen

Pit Stop

Let your friends and coworkers know you are looking to celebrate small wins. Get them on board and create a culture of celebration with your community!

Give high fives to yourself or to a friend at least three times this week.

MEET YOUR MONEY
EXIT 14

"Money is a terrible master but an excellent servant."

P.T. BARNUM

"Hey, Google, play *Celebration*, by Kool & The Gang, on YouTube music." The music starts to play, I get out of the chair in my home office and start to dance. "Celebrate good times, come on" plays, and I sing along as I slide across my laminate flooring to my living room, bouncing around and playfully petting my dog Maggie to encourage her to join in the fun. You are probably wondering what could cause all this excitement? Did I just close a big client or book a huge speaking gig? Or maybe I just hit my sales goal for the year? Nope, it's way better than that. I was getting ready to pay my monthly bills. Ha! I know, by this point in the book, you likely think I am crazy, but this is just one example of me practicing the discipline of celebrating success and turning my frown upside down.

I used to hate paying the bills. We are by no means financially rich, but Keisha and I have always had enough money to cover our bills. Despite that fact, I would dread transferring money toward our student loans, car payments, rent, and the like. To make matters worse, I would spend a significant amount of my time worrying about money in between bill payments, constantly in the rat race of a paycheck-to-paycheck mentality. These worry attacks and the anxiety that I felt when it came to money were the exact opposite of enjoying the grind, so I hope this Exit will help you avoid some of the potholes I drove through when it came to my past relationship with money.

Whether we like to admit it or not, money plays a large role in our lives, so the earlier you can love your money, the better off you will be! Loving your money doesn't mean that money is the only thing that matters in life. It simply means that you build a positive relationship with all of it: the money coming in, the debt you may have from your investment in college, and the way you share it with the world.

STOP SPENDING AND START SHARING

Believe me, anyone who knew me in my twenties would think I was lying if I told them how I celebrate paying my bills. I was one of the most frugal guys you could meet. I was the guy reminding friends they owed me $3.00 from our last trip to Taco Bell, or intentionally not buying lunch, knowing that my friends at the office would always give me their leftovers. If that's not enough to show you how fixed my money mindset was, then here is one final example. At one point in college, someone bet me a couple beers that I wouldn't eat a chicken nugget that had fallen on the floor of our fraternity house. Not only did I eat the chicken nugget, but I vividly remember thinking it was a true win-win. I got two beers *and* a chicken nugget for free! (How far I have come . . .)

I don't tell you any of this about Past Joe because I am proud of it. I share it with you because if I can change my money mindset, then anyone can! It took me a lot of intentional effort, but through reading, journaling, and investing in money mindset coaching, I now have a joy-filled relationship with money, rather than one filled with anger and resentment. I am able to genuinely celebrate sharing my money with people and companies because I take the time to be grateful for what Keisha and I receive in return. When I pay $600 to our car payments, BOOM, another month of driving safe vehicles that we love! Paying $1,700 to our landlord means another month in a great house located in warm and sunny, North Carolina! Sending $1,500 to my business and mindset coaches, hype, that's another six sessions where I can challenge myself, learn, and grow! Let's gooo!

My biggest takeaway is that **money is not something we own, it's something we share.** My twenties were filled with anxiety about paying off my student loans or finding housing that would fit in my budget. I looked at money as something I had but would lose as soon as I purchased something. This feeling of loss became consuming. I felt like I never had enough, and I definitely wasn't appreciating the things, experiences, or peace of mind that my purchasing was giving me. If you have a loving relationship with yourself and are grateful for what you do have, then you can build strong relationships with money and material goods as well.

LOVE YOUR LOANS

As a recent college graduate it is very likely that you are entering the "real-world" with some very real college debt. Whether it's $10,000 or $100,000, it can feel like an overwhelming burden to carry. As you begin making payments, however, I really encourage you to appreciate all the value that comes with those loans.

It kills me when I hear people who speak of their student loans as if they were a *bad* investment. Oftentimes, students walk across the graduation stage and become bitter because they forget what they received from their college experience. Yes, you have a degree, which equipped you with the skills to do the job that you are currently working, but that is just the tip of the iceberg. In most cases, you are sharing your money for the housing that you lived in, the meals you ate, the experiences you had, and most importantly, the person you became in the process. You are you because of how you navigated your college years, and I hope that makes it a bit easier to make your monthly loan payment.

I think this is why I can genuinely dance around my house as I pay my student loan bill (which I am still paying ten years later), because I know that if I didn't invest in my education, then there is no chance of having the life that I love today. I wouldn't have met my amazing professors, coaches, and friends. I wouldn't have gotten to play hockey. I wouldn't have been introduced to my wife! None of it happens if I hadn't taken on student loans. So I am glad to make my payment every month, and I would happily take out the loans again if given the choice.

It is likely that you will pay back your loans over the course of multiple years, so why not enjoy the dozens of payments that you make along the way, and not just the day that you pay them off completely.

SIMPLE INVESTING

I am no expert about how to invest money, but I would be remiss if I didn't mention this to you as you start your career. I remember signing my first contract to work at Adrian College, a week after I graduated, and I didn't have a clue about financial investments. If this is you, check out the resources in the Add to Your Playlist section at the end of this exit. It was my first day and my new employee packet had to be signed by the end of the day. Fortunately for me, a friend and mentor of mine was tasked with walking me through my first day and was in my office as I decided what to do with my retirement contributions. I had the opportunity to start a 403(b), and after two years, the college would match up to a certain percentage of my income. I remember thinking, *I won't even get the match for two years, should I just wait until then to start contributing? I could really use that money now to help get a new car,* and on and on and on. I am paraphrasing here, but he said something to the effect of, "Just put in the max amount now. You'll never miss it, and it can only help you down the road." I checked that box on the form, and that was that.

I realize that we cannot all be as lucky to receive such timely advice or be able to pay the bills easily every month, so I do encourage you to educate yourself on how you can realistically invest in your long-term future based on your current financial status. Most companies and organizations will have an investment plan included in your benefit package, but it's up to you if and how much you pay into it. Take the time to ask questions and consider a low-cost, long-term investment strategy from the very start of your career. The magic of compounding interest is real, and the difference of a couple of years can be the difference in hundreds of thousands of dollars for Future You over the long hall. I know it can seem scary or stressful, but be teachable and lean into the learning process when it comes to your money. Once you are educated on what your options are, you can be empowered to enjoy your relationship with money rather than fear it.

EXIT HERE | MEET YOUR MONEY

Money isn't something we own, it's something we share.

Reframe how you look at your bills and loans. Making payments can be fun when you see what you are receiving in return.

Take the time to learn the basics about investing in your future. A little investing in your early twenties will have huge returns when you retire.

Ask for Directions

What is my current relationship with money?
Do I spend money or share it?
Am I making smart investments now?

Add to Your Playlist

Read this book: *You Are A Badass At Making Money* by Jen Sincero
Read this book: *The Wealthy Barber* by David Chilton
Watch this YouTube video: "Everything You've Been Told About Money is Wrong"

Pit Stop

Take one small step today to learn more about investment opportunities.
Celebrate paying your bills this month.

THINK LIKE A PEAK PERFORMER
EXIT 15

"Your mind needs to be stronger than your feelings . . . Your feelings keep you in bed. Your mind tells you get up."

TIM GROVER

Your thoughts have tremendous influence over your actions and outcomes. Because of this, your mindset and approach to life matters. The energy you choose to bring to a situation dramatically impacts how you experience that moment, so as you drive on the highway of happiness, it is critical that you develop a peak performance mindset so that you can enjoy as many moments as possible. Let's say your mindset is the vehicle that takes you through your life's joy ride. You would want that vehicle to be equipped with features that allow it to perform at its very best. Reliable tires, a powerful engine, and effective brakes would all be must-haves. Here are my must-have mindset concepts that will allow you to default toward action in any situation and crush your twenties.

Must-Have Mindsets on Your Dream Ride

- Every Day Is a Big Day
- Accept the Lows
- Find the Positive
- Live in Abundance

EVERY DAY IS A BIG DAY

In my early twenties, I was an admissions recruiter at Adrian College, and I had the opportunity to present to all the seniors and a few of the juniors at Will Carleton Academy. I walked into the classroom of twelve students and kicked off my presentation like every other.

"Guys... what a day!"

This was a line I used to kick off every presentation because it helped me remember the opportunity I had. I had the opportunity to help high school students get excited about the college process. Proclaiming, "What a day?!" kick-started my energy and allowed me to allude to the infinite possibilities that could come our way. What a day it would be if they applied to college! What a day it would be if they scheduled a visit to tour campus! What a day it would be if they felt just a little bit less stressed about the college search process. This is what I genuinely meant when I proudly proclaimed, "What a day" at the beginning of each of my fifty-plus presentations that fall.

Truth be told, some kids didn't get it. They took it as a frivolous part of my introduction, but to me, it was how I lived my life. But something was different about these kids at Will Carleton Academy. They loved it. They could see it was more than just a phrase, and they bought in. As they completed the free admissions application, they would say, "What a day" as they handed it to me. Over the years, I have given hundreds of college presentations, but I vividly remember my time at Will

Carleton because they matched my energy and they treated my visit like a big day. Their class valedictorian later told me that she kicked off her graduation speech by saying, "Guys, what a day." How cool is that!

Treating every day like it is the biggest day of your life brings perspective and urgency to that day. When you adopt this mindset, you see every day as an opportunity to be your absolute best, and your energy and happiness match that frequency. The question is, will you read this and move on, or will you buy in? If you treat every day like a big day, filled with endless possibilities, then that is exactly what you can expect. You will become more intentional, give more effort, and the results will follow. Don't fall into the trap of becoming complacent at work and in your personal life. Remember that every day is a huge opportunity to bring maximum effort.

Think of your last job interview. That was a big day. That was a day you brought maximum effort. You likely got up early, made breakfast, took a little extra time getting ready, reviewed some interview questions before you hopped in the car. Maybe you even listened to a motivational YouTube video or your favorite hype song to set the tone as you drove into the office. You were early and felt great walking into the interview. Peak performers bring this energy every day. Even after a couple years on the job, they are still coming into the office with that same mentality and vigor as the day they got the job. They treat every day like the interview, so it's no surprise they outperform their colleagues who have become complacent in the mundane routine of daily life.

POTENTIAL ROADBLOCK | WORKING FOR FRIDAY

In your twenties, you will be surrounded by people who are counting the days until Friday. I have a few pet peeves, and this is definitely one of them. You know what you should be pumped for? Tuesday. Or get excited about Thursdays for a change. Why live most of your week just dreaming of the weekend when you could enjoy every day of the week? It makes no sense, yet most people we work with despise Monday through Thursday. You are so freaking lucky to have Monday through Thursday. Give every day the energy and effort it deserves by treating it like a big day. If you are one of the people walking around the office saying, "Thank God it's almost Friday," then really challenge yourself here. Raise your teachability index (See Exit 4) and implement the Every Day is a Big Day mentality from this Exit into your life, and I promise you will see shifts in your energy and motivation levels throughout your weeks.

ACCEPT THE LOWS

Peak performers push themselves beyond their comfort zones. They strive to be their very best, which takes a willingness to go through hardship. As you level up, you need to be prepared for doubt, weakness, pain, fear, and struggle. This is the grind—the hard part about putting your dreams into action. I tell you this because you deserve the truth. The road to accomplishing your dreams is paved through difficulty. If you have the pleasure of living a fully lived experience, then you will inevitably have to work through lows moments.

It is not your responsibility to avoid these emotions; it is actually the opposite. You must be ready to accept the difficulty. Being a peak performer isn't about avoiding the lows or suppressing sadness. Peak performers accept *all* their emotions and honor them in the moment. **Accepting our emotions and navigating lows in a healthy way is a critical component of self-care and a major contributing factor to peak performance.** When you embrace sadness and pain, you give yourself a chance to experience it, grow from it, and move forward.

Enjoying the grind isn't just about feeling happy all the time, it's about experiencing all that life has to offer. Life is full of lows, and when you can accept this truth, rather than resist it, you can work through the low points more effectively. In fact, this is so important to peak performance, I spent all of Exit 16, providing specific strategies to help you work through low moments so you can shorten the time you spend in those emotional states.

Accepting doubt, fear, and sadness doesn't make you weak; rather, it allows you the strength to reach your highest potential. That inner strength and resiliency is what empowers you to be authentic. If you accept all the emotional states that come with growth, then you can be genuine and authentic in your pursuit of joy and success.

FIND THE POSITIVE

Just like you can choose joy, you can choose to see the positive in any situation. As mentioned before, I know you are going to go through difficult times, but once you accept and work through those lows, you need to master the mindset of getting out of that space. Identifying the positive isn't "fluff" or "woo," it's a legitimate tool to bring you back to a peak performance state. As soon as you have given the feeling the respect it deserves, then I encourage you to find the positive within the situation you are presented with. This is easier said than done, but if you gravitate towards gratitude and look for perspective, you can find "good" in any circumstance. To help me with this process I use a technique I refer to as laughable gratitude.

Use Laughable Gratitude

The activity is simple. When you catch yourself getting down or having a negative lens on a situation, immediately think of the exact opposite of the thought you are having, until it becomes laughable.

Event: You are bummed out because your car has a flat tire. Your initial thoughts:

- At least I have a car.
- There are so many people that don't have a car.
- This flat tire means only a day or two without my car. What a great reminder of how lucky I am most of the time.

That is an awesome shift in mindset, but it's still not laughable. Let's think of the car itself and work our way down until we can get a laugh.

- We have access to a vehicle that allows us to travel autonomously across the country at any moment of our lives.
- We can go wherever we want literally whenever we want!
- How lucky are we to have the chance to get a flat tire?!
- People 200 years ago would have killed for the chance to have a flat tire!

Just thinking of people in the 1800s spending days traveling to the market on foot or horseback makes me chuckle. If you want to be happy, you need to default to seeing the positive in situations rather than the negative. Make the choice to see the positive!

LIVE IN ABUNDANCE

People think they are lucky to find a four-leaf clover. Actually they are pretty lucky, as there is a 1 in 10,000 chance of finding one. Knowing these odds, my wife Keisha and I agreed that finding one would go on our bucket list. We would look as we took the dogs on walks and as we visited different parks and trails. We'd suddenly stop during a walk around the neighborhood just to look in a patch of clovers near my neighbor's mailbox. We were determined, but this went on for months with no success.

Then one day while measuring out our future concrete patio, Keisha bent down and noticed a patch of clovers in our backyard. Lo and behold, she found a four-leaf clover! I went *nuts*! I was so pumped! And then we found another . . . and another . . . until we found five in total. We couldn't believe it. Like literally couldn't believe it. I vividly remember running inside like a child to google "four-leaf clovers" to make sure we were looking at the right thing.

A couple days later, I checked the area again. With a fresh set of eyes, I came across a few more. The next day, we found eleven more and two that were five-leaf clovers. Something we hadn't even considered before. With four-leaf clovers being so rare, I had never opened my mind to the possibility of the existence of a five-leaf clover, much less finding two of them!

Without even knowing it, I was limiting myself. I was settling for what I thought was possible, rather than seeing all the options. Peak performers have the skill of defaulting to abundance. There is never any hurdle that can stand in their way and never a limit to what they can achieve. Here are some quick takeaways that I took from this lucky encounter.

One | We often don't believe that good things can happen to us. We feel undeserving or unfit to receive them. Part of peak performance is being open and accepting to allow great things to happen.

Two | When you are open to endless possibilities, you are far more likely to see opportunities coming your way. There are always infinite positive possibilities to experience if we are open to it.

Three | Don't overlook your own backyard. For months, Keisha and I looked in other parks, trails, and clover patches for the four-leaf clover, but we never once focused on our yard. Joy is right in front of you. It can be found in your current job, your current life, your current backyard! Spend less time looking at what others have, and it creates the time to find the joy in what is directly in front of you!

This mindset shift of defaulting to abundance has been the most difficult to implement in my life. I had made a habit of considering how unlikely results were and how scarce resources could be. After finding that five-leaf clover, I have become aware of how natural it was for me to default to scarcity. While I had a positive attitude while starting new endeavors, I was limited to the outcomes that I thought were attainable. I assumed things wouldn't work out, and I would let potential future outcomes deter me from taking realistic steps forward. I was putting a cap on what was possible because I lacked proof in my experience up to that point. As an entrepreneur, I have really focused on improving my abundance mindset and I have already come across many more five-leaf clover moments, and I hope you begin to encounter them as well!

EXIT HERE | THINK LIKE A PEAK PERFORMER

Road Map Recap

Treat every day like it is the biggest day of your life.

Accept and respect all emotional states you experience. The highs *and* the lows.

Find the positive in every situation and interaction.

Live in abundance. Believe there is always more out there for you.

Ask for Directions

Am I treating today like the biggest day of my life?

Am I resisting any negative emotions right now? If so, how can I accept them?

What is one positive of this situation?

Am I acting through abundance or scarcity?

Add to Your Playlist

Read this book: *Focus on the Good Stuff* by Mike Robbins

Read this book: *Stop Doing That Sh*t* by Gary John Bishop

Pit Stop

Use laughable gratitude one time this week to see how it changes your perspective and mood.

FEEL GOOD NOW
EXIT 16

"You cannot stop the waves, but you can learn to surf."

JON KABAT-ZINN

A major part of enjoying the grind is being happy in the moment. Feeling good now. The early years of your career will give you plenty of obstacles and difficulties, so it is important that you are prepared. It will be impossible to avoid setbacks, hard times, and uncertainty, but we can learn how to handle difficult times now for when they arise. We don't always have to feel great or filled with joy, but having tools to feeling better from moment to moment is within our control. To assist you as you evolve, I want to give you three specific actions you can take that will allow you to *work through* your emotions and feel good now in any situation. In their book, *It Takes What It Takes*, Trevor Moawad and Andy Staples point out that there is power in neutral thinking. Ironically enough, he relates shifting states of mental being to shifting gears in your car. He points out that it's impossible to shift from reverse to drive without first shifting from reverse to neutral. My Feel Good Now tool kit is how I shift from reverse to neutral. These strategies allow me to authentically get to a place where I can eventually shift to drive and choose joy.

Being happy is a constant process that takes attention and effort. It can be hard work. Yes, I said it. You have to be willing to do the work to get the result you want. For me, doing the work is journaling, meditating, and being intentionally grateful. These practices can be slow at times, but working through them always makes me feel better than I did before I started. To me, all three of these actions bring us perspective, which leads to wholeness. They are processes that allow us to become aware of how lucky we are in that moment, which allows us to adjust our expectations and be more content.

GET GRATEFUL

I truly want you to be happy and have access to joy at any moment of your life, and to me, being grateful is the spare tire that every vehicle needs to reach your destination. Even when things go wrong, you have that spare tire to rely on to get you out of a jam.

Being grateful is hard because it pushes us to be empathetic and see how fortunate we are. What is difficult about this is that our perspective is based on the people and things that we surround ourselves with daily. To use an extreme example, if you are a millionaire and you are surrounded by other millionaires, you are less likely to be grateful for money because you have access to it and so does everyone else around you. I get it, not everyone is a millionaire, but if you are reading this book, then you have definitely hit the lottery when it comes to where you landed in life. I am not insinuating that everything is perfect, or that it has to be, but if you are reading this book, then it means you had the financial resources to purchase it and free time that you get to spend reading. Sure, in the United States this doesn't seem like much, but there are literally millions of people who don't have access to clean drinking water or functioning toilets. All the while, you and I have access to books and the free time to read them for pleasure. We are insanely lucky. And the more we practice gratitude intentionally, the more we get to see how fortunate we are, and the more humble we become.

There are a lot of ways to become grateful, with an endless amount of things to be grateful for. For me, I write down one thing I am grateful for every day, and I challenge myself to not write the same thing twice. This way, I always start my day off with appreciation and a grateful mindset.

LINK GRATEFULNESS TO DIFFICULTY

Starting off the day with gratitude puts us in peak performance state, but it doesn't always sustain us throughout the day. We will experience pain, anger, frustration, and myriad emotions throughout the day, so it's important to accept those feelings and then use gratitude to improve our mood. Gratitude can relieve some of the tension associated with negativity for physical and emotional experiences, so try your best to take additional time to be grateful in your lowest moments to help you get back to a neutral state.

Laughable Gratitude | Take Two

Like most humans, I used to hate stubbing my toe. Especially in the morning when I was just waking up. Then, in a practice of gratitude, I realized how *lucky* I was to even have toes to stub. I think stubbed toes exist to remind us once in a while to wake up and realize we have it pretty damn good. The question is, are you receiving these reminders, or are letting the pain distract you from the big picture? Let's see it in action.

Event: You stub your toe, leading to immediate pain and anger.

Initial thoughts:

- Think of how lucky you are to have a toe.
- In order to have stubbed it, you had to stub it on something, so you can also be grateful you have that item. This could be a nightstand, coffee table, you name it. At one point you bought that item, with money that you had, so that's awesome.
- You only stub your toe while walking, so this means you can walk. *You can freaking walk . . .*
- You can walk because your brain sends signals to your legs and feet without you consciously thinking about it.
- You have a brain . . . one of the largest and most powerful brains on earth!

Today if Keisha or I stub our toe, it almost always ends with a laugh, as we both rush to yell out, "At least you have a toe!" It hurts way less and we get over it way faster because we focus on how unbelievably fortunate we are in that moment. We all know we can get trapped in downward spirals, but I am here to tell you that you can literally create your own upward spirals using laughable gratitude. If you can't see the joy and humor, then I really suggest you revisit Exit 3, because you are missing the power of always choosing joy.

Stubbing a toe is a lighthearted example, but this same theory can be applied to the big things in life as well. When you make gratitude a daily practice, it prepares you for the big tests that life will throw at you. Whether it is a serious relationship ending, a loved one falling ill, or the passing of someone close, all these things are part of the human experience. I want to be clear that gratefulness isn't a substitute for grieving, but it is a tool that you can use to provide perspective and assist you to work through your emotions in a healthy and productive way.

Just like stubbing your toe, the shift in perspective doesn't stop the pain, but it does allow you to get to a space of neutral thinking and eventually feel better faster. Humans are complex creatures with the ability to feel multiple emotions at once. When we are faced with tragedy, it is okay to allow yourself to feel grateful amid the pain. Gratitude won't instantly cure sadness, but it can be an effective tool to help lighten the load.

WRITE IT OUT

Another way to feel good now is to journal. Writing out our thoughts is a healthy and productive way to process our emotions. The act of getting them out of our minds and onto paper is empowering. Our thoughts can play tricks on us, but writing them out gives us the ability to see them for what they truly are. Typically, this helps us gain perspective and understand that what we are going through is temporary and will pass. I have been journaling for a couple of years now, and here are some of my favorite ways to find happiness through journaling.

Free Writing. Free writing is a helpful practice that allows you a safe space to share, vent, and reflect. There doesn't always have to be a big breakthrough at the end, and there's no pressure to find an "aha" moment. The act of writing is enough. Just write about whatever comes up for you.

Dream Writing. Writing out our dreams and desires makes it more likely they will come to fruition. Write out things that you want to accomplish, or list physical possessions that you want to acquire. This can be a fun exercise to keep you motivated and energized as you put in the effort needed to manifest your desired outcomes. Now that I have a couple of journals filled with previous aspirations that have become reality, it's extremely empowering to continue this practice. I have so much proof of my dreams coming true that it's hard not to write them down now.

Write a Letter Or Quick Note. I strongly recommend this method for any relationship that you want to improve in your life. Writing forgiveness or apology letters can free you of past heartaches and old narratives that are holding you back from reaching your true potential. Whether you actually send the letter is completely up to you, because writing the letter can be freeing enough! Sometimes it can even give you the courage (and the words) to have the conversation with that person in real life. Or you may choose to never bring it up to that person, and that's okay too. If you are looking to improve your relationship with inanimate things like money, your job, or your mindset, this is also a powerful practice. The structure of a letter allows you to get your thoughts and feelings out of your head and on to the page!

Use a Prompt. There are thousands of journal prompts out there. From directed questions to writing out affirmations, utilizing prompts can be a powerful way to overcome a specific roadblock. You can search them on google, or create your own questions, but don't be afraid to utilize guided prompts.

As a performance coach, and someone who has invested in my own coaching, I know how powerful it can be to have someone else to bounce ideas off. Whether it is investing in a coach or therapist, or calling up a friend, having someone to listen to you and troubleshoot problems and opportunities with is critical to development. To me, journaling is the greatest form of self-coaching you can perform. By writing things out and rereading them, you can see yourself authentically. In this way, you can act as your own listener and carry out a dialogue and discourse with yourself. Grab a journal and a pen and write it out! You won't regret it!

MIX IN MEDITATION

Three minutes. That is the amount of time I spent on meditation when I first began practicing. I committed myself to meditating for three minutes every single day before I would do yoga. Two years later, I am up to ten minutes a day. Yup, two years have passed, and I increased my tolerance by seven whole minutes! Better watch out, here I come!

Kidding aside, I mention this because I want to share with you the power of meditation on a really small scale. There is a ton of science and hundreds of years of evidence showing meditation helps reduce stress, increase clarity, and is overall a positive practice for our mental health. For years, I never tried it because I thought you had to do it for long durations of time to feel any results. Despite my resistance, I looked for a lay-up and decided to try it for just three minutes. Three minutes of deep breathing for a couple of weeks made a positive impact on my mood, reduced my stress, and helped me with decision-making. With my ADHD and wandering mind, I found that something was better than nothing, which allowed me to increase the length of my meditation practice over time.

The great news is that meditation is no longer reserved for monks and you don't have to sit cross-legged in nature in a holy place. There are countless YouTube videos and meditation apps that walk you through guided meditations to help you get started. You can lie on your back, sit upright in a chair, or even sneak in a little meditation as you ride in the back of an Uber.

For me, the key to implementing meditation was to release my preconceived expectations. Initially, I struggled because I had set high expectations for what meditation was meant to be. With no practice or real understanding of what meditation actually is, I assumed that I should be able to sit in complete silence without any thoughts or distractions for at least twenty to thirty minutes. This would be extremely difficult for anyone who is new to meditation, much less someone with ADHD.

As I lowered my expectations and committed to trying my best for only three minutes, I started to understand that meditation isn't about silence, it's about getting better at hearing what your mind has to say. Jon Kabat-Zinn explained it best when he said, "Meditation is not about feeling a certain way. It's about feeling the way you feel."[1] Once I started looking at meditation this way, the whole thing became soothing rather than frustrating. I would sit down and immediately be bombarded with thoughts. Thoughts that were important, ideas that were irrelevant, reflections about the past, concerns and excitement in relation to the future. I was all over the place, but every time I lost focus, I would bring my attention back to my breath.

This scenario played out for a couple weeks, and I started to work on accepting thoughts as they came in and then intentionally letting them go. I imagined them floating into my awareness, and then floating away so I could get back to my breath. Then I started meditating for four minutes, then five, and so on. Today, I enjoy the calm and presence that I get after ten minutes, and I try to meditate three to four times a week. It's long enough to accept any thoughts that come up for me and experience some healing breathwork, but short enough where I don't feel like I need to rush off to the next thing. I use this time to let my subconscious thoughts present themselves to my conscious mind. I evaluate and let go of concerns and fear, I laugh at musings, and I make note of ideas or concepts that I want to add to my calendar. I accept all of it for what it is, and it allows me to live more in the present throughout the day.

Start out small, enjoy the process, and mix in meditation when you can!

EXIT HERE | FEEL GOOD NOW

Road Map Recap

Daily practice of gratitude allows us to see life as a gift rather than a burden.

Journaling is a healthy and productive way to respect your feelings and navigate roadblocks that come your way.

Even a few minutes of meditation on a daily basis can lead to improvements in your mood. Stick with it and don't get discouraged early on!

Ask for Directions

How do I currently process difficulties in my life?

Am I willing to try something new, like journaling, meditation, or intentional gratitude to experience my thoughts in a more healthy and effective way?

What do I need to do to feel good now?

Add to Your Playlist

Read this book: *Hardwiring Happiness* by Rick Hanson, PhD

Read this book: *Twelve and a Half* by Gary Vaynerchuk

Watch this YouTube video: "The Long Journey to Becoming '10% Happier'"

Pit Stop

Try meditating twice this week for three minutes.

Try journaling twice this week for ten minutes.

CONNECT WITH COMMUNITY
EXIT 17

"A person does not become whole until he or she becomes a part of something bigger than himself or herself."

JIMMY VALVANO

By now, your dream vehicle is equipped with some major upgrades to allow you to enjoy the highway of happiness. You have a peak performance mindset, ownership of your life, and a loving relationship with yourself. You are making lay-ups along the way, and you are probably feeling like you can pull off to the nearest exit and stop. Fight that urge to settle. Stay steady and push yourself to continue the journey of learning and growth. Again, you can drive slowly, but always keep moving.

Remember, your relationship with yourself is the foundation for every relationship you have in your life. Now that you have put in the work and your foundation is solid, you have the opportunity to share some of the joy with others! Until now, the entire book has been about you and how to navigate stress and create happiness by yourself. While it's critical to be able to experience happiness alone, true happiness is amplified when it is shared with others. Relationships with others greatly enhance our life and provide a major opportunity to find joy and purpose throughout the grind.

That said, your twenties can become a turbulent time and managing relationships can become overwhelming. You are expected to maintain old friendships from high school and college, establish new connections with colleagues and coworkers, and if you are lucky maybe find a significant other. Oh yeah, and you could have your siblings, parents, grandparents, cousins, aunts, uncles too, don't forget them. And none of those people are as easy to keep in contact with if you move away. As you can see, it's complicated, so before you let a bunch of people into your car and hit the open road, you need to get a better sense of who you should let in and how you should treat them along the trip.

Unfortunately, in my twenties, I didn't know how to balance it all, so I did the most reasonable thing I could think of at the time: I buried myself in my work and acted like everything was fine. After college, I wasn't able to visit home or hang out with friends as often as I anticipated. Friends were taking jobs farther away, getting married, having kids, and it just got to be overwhelming. To me, there were roadblocks and construction zones popping up left and right. I felt like such a bad friend, so I gave up entirely. I attended the few gatherings I could, rarely texted or called, and I blamed my busy work schedule every chance I got. I didn't admit it to myself at the time, but I know it was my fault those relationships weren't maintained. Deep down I felt horrible for how I was showing up for others. This is why I encourage you to keep driving and push yourself to make the time for the people you care about. Yes, it feels overwhelming at times, but you have shown that you can show up for yourself, so find a way to show up for the people in your community.

JOE'S DICTIONARY

Community: Everyone around you. It's your parents, siblings, friends, coworkers, the clients your company serves, and the guy next to you in the Target checkout line. And yes, all those cousins, aunts, and uncles too. It's all the people you have access to.

Seeing everyone as your community reminds you that we are all connected and we can always be a proactive participant in our community. It can be as big or small as we decide it is, and it can grow as much as we allow it to. The exciting part is that it's up to us to create a community and decide how we show up for others.

A LITTLE EVERY DAY GOES A LONG WAY

This is where I went wrong in my twenties: I grossly misunderstood what it meant to show up for people. I thought that being a good friend only meant hanging out on the weekend or seeing each other in person. As friends moved away to start their careers and families of their own, I failed to realize the impact of a text, FaceTime call, Venmo transaction, or even a like on Instagram. You can't sustain good friendships just leaving likes on Instagram, but small interactions can allow you to encourage and support your friends during the months and sometimes years that you don't get to see each other in person. I always felt bad because I didn't go on many trips with friends or make it to all my family gatherings, and I worried they judged me for not attending. This assumption caused me to distance myself further, which led me to doing nothing rather than something. In life, *something is always better than nothing*, and that holds true with maintaining relationships.

I didn't keep in touch much with my parents or family back home, I did very little outside of work, and most of my actions were based on what I needed or wanted at the time. I had become the friend who only called if they needed something, and I hated that about myself.

Something had to change, so I found a lay-up and I started small. Every day for the last four years, I have tried to do something for someone in my community. I couldn't always be there for everyone, but I realized that I could contribute to others regularly. So, I started doing one act of kindness for someone else each day. These were things like text an old friend, check in on a staff member, open a door for a stranger, etc. Weeks and months passed, and I became amazed at how many people there were to do small acts of kindness for. Seeing the world through this lens has allowed me to see opportunities that went beyond my immediate friends and family. Through the years, I have reached out to people I barely knew to compliment them, or to create a new connection. I have collaborated with people that were once outside my current community, and I definitely have deepened relationships that already existed. We live in such a unique time where we don't have to be physically near someone to encourage them, support them, or connect with them, and I have noticed a big difference when I take advantage of that ability to reach out. Sending a hype text to a friend who has a big day ahead of them or sending a couple bucks via Venmo to buy a coffee for a friend to celebrate one of their accomplishments are all reasonable things that are within your control. The best part is, these actions will make the people in your community feel loved and supported, and it will light you up too!

It's crazy to think about it now, but four years is 1,460 days. That's more than 1,460 opportunities, interactions, conversations, and connections that I have proactively added to my life in just four years. If you started this when you were twenty-five, you would have contributed to others an additional 18,250 times by the time you turned seventy-five.

Think of how much joy *you* would be sharing with others. Think of the positive difference you could make in the *world*. Think of the *joy!*

Pro Tip from an Awesome Friend

I realize you may not have the bandwidth right now to connect with one person every day, so I wanted to give you this quick tip that I picked up from a close friend of mine, Mackenzie. Her strategy for keeping in touch and serving others is to simply reach out to people as you think of them. If you see a truck that reminds you of your friend from high school, send them a text and ask what's up. If you are in the line at the grocery store and you see a cute little kid in front of you and it reminds you of your friend with a newborn baby, then send her a video message that says hi and you can't wait to visit and meet her little guy. Again, something is better than nothing, so let your own thoughts and memories become opportunities to take action and reach out.

ADOPT A SERVANT'S MENTALITY

When I encourage clients to do things for others on a daily basis, they all do really well in the first couple weeks. The hurdle comes in week three when they have already surprised a couple coworkers with Starbucks and called their dad a couple of times, and they are out of ideas. We can solve this issue by adopting a servant's mentality. I challenge myself and my clients every day to lean into empathy and consider what the people in our community's might need. Think of others and what they may be going through and try to show up for them with a servant mindset. Again, be okay with texting or sending a video message to people. It is a great way to show support and care when you are short on time. It truly is the thought that counts, so show you're thinking of them and that they matter.

The other benefit of coming from a lens of service is that the equation for happiness applies to relationships with others as well. If we expect a ton from others, we will feel let down, sad, or frustrated if they don't meet those expectations. You have to remember they are super busy and trying to navigate this winding road too. If someone forgets to call you or can't make it to your birthday party, have empathy and try not to take it personally. By focusing on serving others without expectations in return, we set ourselves up to be pleasantly surprised, which is a way more enjoyable way to live. If you want powerful, genuine, and joy-filled relationships, then give more than you receive.

SERVICE IN ACTION

Years ago while reading *Leaders Eat Last* by Simon Sinek, I bought into the idea that true leadership comes from serving your people. I started to expect less from my staff and looked for ways to serve them. Rather than expect increases in their effort, I increased my training and support. I added elements to our culture that provided a sense of belonging and family. The cohesiveness within my team changed, our recruitment numbers increased, and team morale increased significantly.

Truth be told, I had fallen in the habit of thinking, *what's in it for me?* which led to consistently being let down. I remember entering into projects or working relationships thinking, *If I do this work, or if I cultivate this relationship, how will it help me?* Boy, did I have it wrong. Seeing myself as a servant helped me put my ego aside and simply help others. When I implemented a service-based action plan, a lot changed for me. Not only were our recruitment efforts successful but more importantly I felt so much better. Trying my best to serve others was a huge step toward enjoying the grind in my professional life and has become the fuel in my personal life as well.

EXIT HERE | CONNECT WITH COMMUNITY

Road Map Recap

We are in control of how we contribute to our community and show up for others.

When it comes to relationships, something is always better than nothing.

One act of kindness a day can lead to thousands of life-changing interactions over a lifetime.

Ask for Directions

Who can I serve today?

Am I expecting too much of a friend or coworker in this situation?

Add to Your Playlist

Read this book: *Elevate your Network* by Jake Kelfer

Read this book: *The Fine Art of Small Talk* by Debra Fine

Pit Stop

Do one act of service for someone in your community today.

FINISH WHAT YOU START
EXIT 18

"Many will start fast, few will finish strong."

GARY RYAN BLAIR

In 1968, John Stephen Akhwari headed to Mexico City to represent his home country of Tanzania in the summer Olympic games as a marathon runner. Unfortunately, Akhwari would suffer a fall during the race. His right leg was badly cut, and he dislocated his knee. Medical personnel bandaged up his leg and determined that he would need further treatment and should go to the hospital immediately. Against their advice, Akhwari started down the road behind the rest of the other runners. Given the severity of his injuries, he wasn't able to run. Through a combination of jogging, hobbling, and walking, he pushed ahead. Two hours and twenty minutes after the race had started, the first runner crossed the finish line to win the gold medal. Akhwari was nowhere close.

To make matters worse, Mexico City is brutal on marathon runners. At just under 7,400 feet in altitude, the air has roughly

23 percent less oxygen than at sea level. Eighteen of the seventy-four competitors didn't finish the race that day. Eighteen of the world's best runners didn't finish, but John Stephen Akhwari was determined not to be one of them. An hour later, followed by a police escort, and clearly in a great deal of pain, he finished the race. When reporters asked why he put himself through all that agony to finish, he responded with this, "My country didn't send me five thousand miles to start a race. They sent me five thousand miles to finish it."

John Stephen Akhwari perfectly exemplifies the mindset of a peak performer and committing to finishing everything you start. In the next few years, you are going to be riddled with hurdles and potential excuses to stop pursuing peak performance. As you venture off on your own, you will be faced with more decisions than at any other point in your life thus far. It is very common for people to start many things, but they lack the discipline to see them through. They start multiple races but finish very few because they take on too much at once and they don't place enough value on completing something before they start something new. This leads to juggling too many things and experiencing mediocre results across the board. Not only is this a recipe for frustration, but it also ensures average results at work and in life. After a few months of this balancing act, people burn out and lack motivation to complete even the simplest of tasks, which creates more excuses to not finish rather than proof that finishing is a reward within itself. This cycle is very easy to fall into, but it can be broken if you stay committed to finishing what you start. A great way to ensure that you are able to finish what you start is to become protective of your time and be aware of what you are committing to in the first place. Just like John, you will have moments where you want to quit, but in those moments, it is paramount to push yourself through the excuses and the short-term pain to finish. Your excuses are valid, and your pain is real, but giving up won't allow you to experience the results you want. You can respect your feelings and keep pushing. It doesn't have to be one or the other. I promise, the short-term pain and tension that you feel will be worth it, because finishing what you set out to start builds a long-term positive association with yourself, which outweighs short-term pain.

SETTING BOUNDARIES | WHEN ENOUGH IS ENOUGH

If you utilize the WIN question you learned in Exit 7, you should be able to prioritize important tasks and use your time effectively to get everything done. If you are still having issues, then it's likely you don't have a time management problem. You have a problem with setting boundaries and have taken too much on. If you are in a position of leadership, then these are the tasks that you delegate and entrust to your team. If you are still working your way up the ladder or it's something personal that you have on your to-do list, it may be time to set up a meeting with your boss or talk to your spouse or friend about setting realistic expectations. Having tasks delegated to you is a form of trust, so it is great news to be receiving so many opportunities, but it is important to open the lines of communication at work and at home if you are becoming overwhelmed. I know it can be scary to say no, but it is important to communicate when you reach your capacity or anticipate that happening. Remember, happiness is always predicated on our expectations, so establishing healthy boundaries is critical.

Most leaders, family members, or friends are not intentionally trying to burn us out, but they will keep relying on you until you establish boundaries. Until you communicate overwhelm and say no to things, it's impossible for your team leader to realize that you're at your capacity. Being honest with yourself when you can do more and honest with your team when you are doing too much can allow everyone to feel and perform better in the long run.

HOW TO BREAK THE CYCLE OF OVERCOMMITMENT

Early in your career, you will make a lot of new relationships in a relatively quick amount of time. Countless opportunities will present themselves to you, and you can feel obligated to say yes to everything. Your intentions are good because you want to please people in your life, but overcommitment is what leads to a juggling act in the first place. Everyone has the intention to finish what they start, but unfortunately, they take on too many things at the same time.

Slow Down and Pause Before You Say Yes

Before you commit, take a little time to think through what that additional commitment would entail. Consider everything else on your calendar and see *if and how* it could fit in your schedule. Make sure you also consider the sacrifices that you would need to make to see it through. Some things will be easier than others to add to your schedule, and some will be more in your control, but if you want to climb the ladder, you need to become someone who finishes everything you start. You need to be someone that your manager, peers, and community can count on to get the job done—and done well. Be impeccable with your words. When you say you can have the report on your boss's desk by Friday, get it done. When you set a time to have drinks with friends, make sure to be there. When you set up a meeting with someone else in your department, respect their time by showing up on time.

ICING ON THE CAKE

This doesn't mean you have to say no to everything, it just ensures that you can be fully accountable to the endeavors you say yes to. If there is something that you want to do but don't have realistic time in your current schedule, put a note in your calendar to revisit it in a month. You can leave space for it in the future. When I am honest with myself about what I have time to do really well, it gives me the energy to complete it sooner and move on to the next thing, which is an added bonus!

Yes, finishing what we start establishes credibility among our coworkers, which leads to success at work, but there's way more! When we finish what we start, we deliver on promises we made to ourselves. Big or small, being accountable to your commitments establishes integrity and self-worth. That alone will strengthen your relationship with yourself and is a huge form of self-love. Only saying yes to the things we feel 100% aligned with is not selfish, nor does it make you a bad person. It is a natural part of the adult world that as you begin to respect your time more, you will realize how many compromises you will be tempted to make because of what others think of you. If this happens, it's okay. Just work through that season of your life, finish what you started, and learn from it moving forward! This is a process, and it will take time to find the right balance for you. The hope is that you overcommit yourself less and less as the years go on so you can see more and more projects through and enjoy them as you do.

EXIT HERE | FINISH WHAT YOU START

Road Map Recap

It's not about finishing first, it's about finishing every race you start. You can respect the reasons to quit along the way and push forward to finish.

Slow down and pause before you say yes.

Finishing what you start strengthens your relationship with yourself and is a valuable form of self-care.

Ask for Directions

Will this opportunity or event fit into my schedule?

Do I have the bandwidth and interest in seeing this all the way through?

Add to Your Playlist

Read this book: *Finish What You Start* by Peter Hollis

Watch this YouTube video: "The Ultimate Display of Determination! Ft. John Akhwari"

Pit Stop

The next time you are asked to take on a new task or commit to a new endeavor, pause and ask yourself, *Is this something I can see through to the end?*

HIT THE ROAD

CONCLUSION

"You do not rise to the level of your goals. You fall to the level of your systems."

JAMES CLEAR

On February 24, 2022, I was twenty-three days into writing the first draft of this book. It was a Wednesday. I coach my clients on Mondays and Tuesdays, so Wednesdays were writing days. Being the lover of alliteration that I am, I even went as far as calling them Writing Wednesdays to clearly define my intentions. This particular morning, however, had become Waste the Day on Instagram Wednesday. I had blocked five minutes to post my Instagram story, but that had quickly turned into forty-five minutes of scrolling, procrastinating, and yes, major time wasting.

As a performance coach, times like these can be extra difficult for me because I know better. Then I get down on myself for getting distracted, which can trigger, yet again, more time wasting. I knew I just needed to grab my laptop and start writing. I knew I would find my flow, and I knew that taking action was the only thing that would actually help me feel better about the book. I knew *what* to do, but man, I did not want to do it.

The truth is, after twenty-three days of writing, I had written all the "easy" chapters. I had been able to find motivation early on because of the excitement that accompanies starting a new project. The honeymoon phase of writing had worn off, the skeleton of the first draft was done, and the real work was about to begin: I needed to fill in chapters that were a little more difficult to write. I had to start making the decisions of what content to keep and what to delete. I was leveling up. I was getting one step closer to my highest potential, and I was scared of the work that would come with it. Once again, I knew what to do, but I had to get myself to actually do it.

So I did.

I grabbed my laptop, started writing, and I finished what I started.

DO WHAT YOU KNOW

By reading this entire book, you have added so many features to assist you on your journey. You now have the capacity to immediately take your personal life, happiness, and career to the next level. The question is, will you take action and *do* anything about it? Knowing *what* to do and actually *doing* it are very different. If you want to enjoy the grind, you have to live a life of action. So what's it going to be? Are you going to be one of the people who implements the disciplines and creates their own unique success or are you going to be someone who says, "I know, I know," but doesn't do anything about it?

LET'S GOOO!

If you want to leave a positive impact in this world and love the life you are living, you need to have a system. A framework that will guide you toward action. Consider these eighteen disciplines as the foundation of that framework. They are a road map of *what to do*, but it's up to you to act. Just like me starting to write this book, you are going to have times where things are flowing. Certain disciplines will come easily, and you'll implement them right away. Work through those first few to gain momentum so you can push yourself as you move on to disciplines outside your comfort zone. The day that you feel that tension, look for a lay-up, hang the lights, and take on the next challenge. It is in those moments where you will find your deepest sense of joy.

As you level up and drive through different seasons of your life, lean into the eighteen disciplines to give yourself what you need. You will encounter bad weather and difficult conditions, so be ready to create your own motivation and remember you *can* get yourself through any storm. Always be teachable and think like a peak performer, and be receptive to new ideas and willing to accept change. The next few years will become stressful at times, so make sure to slow down, reflect often, and celebrate wins—big and small. Respect yourself and your body and I promise, Future You will thank you later! Accept the lows and be grateful for everything you experience along your journey so you can feel good now.

Love yourself, choose happiness, and share with your community.

Hit the open road and enjoy the grind!

NOTES

THE 18 DISCIPLINES

1. Jocko Willink, *Discipline Equals Freedom: Field Manual Mk1-MOD1* (Manhattan, New York City: St. Martin's Press, 2020).

LOVE YOURSELF

1. Michael Neill, *Super Coach* (Carlsbad, California: Hay House Inc., 2018), 43.
2. Mel Robbins, *The 5 Second Rule* (New York City, NY: Savio Republic, 2017).

FIND YOUR FOCUS

1. Tim Bilyeu, "He Explains in 51 Seconds Everything That's Holding You Back | Les Brown on Impact Theory," YouTube video, January 14, 2020, https://www.youtube.com/watch?v=PeK9EeKNXDM.

CHOOSE JOY

1. "Joy," *Merriam-Webster's Unabridged Dictionary*, Merriam-Webster, May 8, 2022, https://unabridged.merriam-webster.com/unabridged/joy.
2. "Happiness," *Merriam-Webster's Unabridged Dictionary*, Merriam-Webster, May 8, 2022, https://unabridged.merriam-webster.com/unabridged/happiness.
3. Mo Gawdat, Solve for Happy (Manhattan, NY: Gallery Books, 2017).
4. The Diary of a CEO, "The Happiness Expert That Made 51 Million People Happier: Mo Gawdat | E101," YouTube video, October 10, 2021, https://www.youtube.com/watch?v=csA9YhzYvmk.
5. Milja Milenkovic, "42 Worrying Workplace Stress Statistics," The American Institute of Stress, September 25, 2019, https://www.stress.org/42-worrying-workplace-stress-statistics#:~:text=In%202019%2C%2094%25%20of%20American,experiencing%20stress%20at%20their%20workplace.&text=According%20to%20Wrike's%20United%20States,of%20stress%20were%20unreasonably%20hig h
6. "Stress," Mental Health Foundation, updated September 17, 2021, https://www.mentalhealth.org.uk/a-to-z/s/stress.

NOTES

ALWAYS BE TEACHABLE

1. Kevin Trudeau, "Your Wish Is Your Command," episode 1, audio series on SoundCloud, 2018.
2. Leo Tolstoy, *War and Peace*, trans. Aylmer Maude and Louise Maude (independently published, 2020).

WORK FOR FUTURE YOU

1. Trevor Moawad and Andy Staples, *It Takes What It Takes: How to Think Neutrally and Gain Control of Your Life* (San Francisco, California: Harper One, 2020).
2. David Goggins, *Can't Hurt Me* (Carson City, NV: Lioncrest Publishing, 2018).
3. Passion 4 Creativity, "You DO what is EASY, Your Life will be HARD!! | LES BROWN," YouTube video, September 17, 2020, https://www.youtube.com/watch?v=uMUkgVp8KxU.

WIN THE DAY

1. Morning Lifter, "Jim Rohn—Don't Major in MINOR Things," YouTube video, August 3, 2020, https://www.youtube.com/watch?v=LQPvSd6NGiY.

LOOK FOR LAY-UPS

1. Dan Coyle, *The Talent Code*, 1st ed. (New York City, NY: Bantam Books, 2009).

RISE AND GRIND

1. Shawn Stevenson, *Sleep Smarter* (Emmaus, Pennsylvania: Rodale Books, 2016).
2. Stevenson, *Sleep Smarter*.

REFLECT EVERY WEEK

1. "How to Focus Better," Tony Robbins (website), accessed May 7, 2022, https://www.tonyrobbins.com/how-to-focus/.

NOTES

CELEBRATE SUCCESS

1. Nicole Spector, "Smiling can trick your brain into happiness—any boost your health," Better by Today, *NBC News*, January 9, 2018, https://www.nbcnews.com/better/health/smiling-can-trick-your-brain-happiness-boost-your-health-ncna822591.

FEEL GOOD NOW

1. Jon Kabat-Zinn, *Wherever You Go, There You Are* (New York City, NY: Hachette Books, 2005).

ACKNOWLEDGMENTS

To my wife, Keisha. Thank you for your endless support and unconditional love as I pursue my dreams. You have truly allowed me to enjoy the grind, and for that I am forever grateful.

Thank you to my mom, my accountability coach on this project. I have always admired your love for reading, and sharing this journey with you was such a joy. Thank you for pushing me, encouraging me, and providing well timed GIFs to ensure we both laughed along the way.

Thank you to my dad for teaching me the importance of discipline from a young age and reminding me that fulfillment comes from enjoying the process.

To my close friends and family, thank you for always supporting me and encouraging me. I am so blessed to have you in my life and community, and I have learned so much from you.

To my friends and mentors at Adrian College. I was so fortunate to be surrounded by such amazing people in my twenties, and your love and guidance truly shaped me into the person I am today. I look back at my time at Adrian with fond memories and am extremely Bulldog Proud.

A special shoutout to George Holton for your unwavering support from day one. You are a great lawyer, peak-performing client, and a better friend. I also want to send a little extra love to my friend Bryan Pike, my first paying client. Thank you for investing in my coaching back in March of 2020. That day literally changed my life, and I am forever grateful for your friendship.

Thank you to Jake Kelfer, my book coach, for providing the road map to writing and launching my own book and for the support to bring it all to life. Thank you for believing in me.

Thank you to M-T, my mindset coach, for teaching me to trust my authority and lean into the things that serve me. Writing this book constantly challenged me, and your persistence and guidance gave me the confidence to share it with others. Thanks for being my mirror.

Thank you to Shaun Surgener, for showing me how to live life on my terms. Leaving my nine-to-five all started with your guidance and encouragement, and I am so grateful for your coaching and support early on.

To my editor, Carly Catt. Thank you for your input, suggestions, and flexibility on this project. I am so grateful for your help in taking this book to the next level.

Finally I want to thank you, the readers. I am so grateful for your time, energy, and attention. Thank you for allowing me to be along for the ride as you cruise the highway of happiness, and thank you for making time to enjoy the grind!

ABOUT THE AUTHOR

Joe Van Geison is a peak performance coach, master motivator, and dynamic speaker who has inspired countless people to create joy and find success in their personal and professional lives. After a fruitful nine-year career in higher education, Joe founded Focus Solutions, a Peak Performance company and developed his signature FOCUS Philosophy. Joe helps his clients reach their highest potential and find joy in their lives by drawing on his years of experience working with elite performers.

Joe lives in North Carolina with his amazing wife Keisha and their two loveable dogs, Maggie, and Rue. When he is not connecting with others, you can find Joe on the golf course, a hiking trail, or paddle boarding at a nearby lake.

Learn more at www.focussolutionscoaching.com

 instagram.com/joevangeison
linkedin.com/in/joe-van-geison-64771a82

Made in the USA
Middletown, DE
26 March 2023

27652163R00099